ART DIRECTORS' INDEX TO ILLUSTRATORS No. 8

ART DIRECTORS' INDEX TO ILLUSTRATORS No. 8

Dust jacket photo and design Photo et design de la jaquette Foto und Gestaltung des Schutzumschlages	Bertram Bahner, Bonn	
Divider page design Design des pages de titres Design der Länder-Seiten	Adrian Hodgkins, Oxford	
Production manager Chef de production Produktionsleiter	Bernard Vouillamoz, Geneva	
Publisher Editeur Verlag	RotoVision SA Case postale 434 10, rue de l'Arquebuse CH-1211 Geneva 11 Tel. 022-21 21 21 Telex: 421 479 rovi ch Fax: 22/29 91 72 From March 1988: 9, route de Suisse CH-1295 Mies Tél. 22-55 30 55 Fax: 22-55 40 72	
Copyright	© 1988 RotoVision SA ISBN 2-88046-070-0	

All rights reserved. No part of this book may be reproduced in any form or by any electronic or mechanical means including information storage and retrieval systems without permission in writing from the publisher, except by a reviewer who may quote brief passages in a review.
This book is sold subject to the condition that it shall not be distributed by way of trade or otherwise be circulated without the publisher's prior consent. All transparencies and/or photographs and/or illustrations reproduced in the book have been accepted on the condition that they are reproduced with the knowledge and prior consent of the photographer and/or illustrator concerned and no responsibility is accepted by the Publisher or Printer for any infringement of copyright or otherwise arising out of publication thereof.
The work of this index is the choice of the Artists and/or their representatives, not of the Publisher.
As this book is printed in four-colour process, a few of the illustrations reproduced here may appear to be slightly different than in their original reproduction.

Tous droits réservés. Ce livre ne peut en aucune manière être reproduit en tout ou partie, sous quelque forme que ce soit ou encore par des moyens mécaniques ou électroniques, y compris le stockage des données et leur retransmission par voie de l'informatique sans l'autorisation par écrit de l'éditeur, le droit de citation à des fins de critiques étant toutefois réservé.
L'ouvrage est vendu sous condition qu'en aucun cas il ne pourra être distribué sans l'accord de l'éditeur. Les diapositives et/ou les photographies et/ou illustrations reproduites dans l'ouvrage ont été acceptées à la condition qu'elles soient reproduites avec l'accord préalable des photographes et/ou des illustrateurs concernés; en conséquence, l'éditeur ou l'imprimeur n'encourt aucune responsabilité ayant sa cause dans une violation du droit d'auteur ou de tout autre droit de propriété intellectuelle résultant de la parution de l'ouvrage.
Le choix des matières dans cet index est le fait des artistes et/ou de leurs représentants et non de l'éditeur.
Ce livre étant imprimé en quadrichromie, de légères différences avec la reproduction originale peuvent apparaître dans certains cas.

Alle Rechte vorbehalten. Kein Teil dieses Buches darf ohne schriftliche Genehmigung des Herausgebers in irgendeiner Form bzw. durch irgendwelche elektronische oder mechanische Mittel — einschliesslich der Systeme zur Speicherung und Wiedergewinnung von Information — reproduziert werden, ausser durch einen Kritiker, der in einer Rezension kurze Abschnitte zitieren darf.
Dieses Buch darf ohne vorherige Genehmigung des Verlages in keiner Form im Handel oder anderswo in Umlauf gebracht werden. Alle in diesem Buch verwendeten Diapositive und/oder Fotografien und/oder Illustrationen sind unter der Bedingung angenommen worden, dass sie mit Wissen und vorheriger Genehmigung des jeweiligen Fotografen und/oder Illustrators reproduziert werden, und Verlag und Druckerei übernehmen keine Verantwortung für eine durch die Veröffentlichung der Bilder entstehende Verletzung des Copyright oder anderen Missbrauch.
Die Arbeit in diesem Buch ist die Wahl der Fotografen/Illustratoren und/oder ihrer Agenten, und nicht des Verlages.
Da dieses Buch im Vierfarbendruck hergestellt ist, können gegenüber der Original-Reproduktion kleinere Differenzen vorkommen.

Contents / Contenu / Inhalt

North America
- 15 United States / Etats-Unis / Vereinigte Staaten
- 145 Canada / Canada / Kanada

South America
- 161 Brazil / Brésil / Brasilien

Asia
- 181 Hong Kong / Hongkong / Hong Kong
- 169 Japan / Japon / Japan

South-East Asia
- 189 Malaysia / Malaisie / Malaysia
- 195 Thailand / Thaïlande / Thailand

Australasia
- 205 Australia / Australie / Australien
- 197 New Zealand / Nouvelle-Zélande / Neuseeland

Europe

Benelux
- 213 Belgium / Belgique / Belgien
- 217 Holland / Hollande / Holland
- 223 Luxembourg / Luxembourg / Luxemburg

- 225 France / France / Frankreich
- 233 Germany / Allemagne / Deutschland
- 281 Spain / Espagne / Spanien
- 209 Turkey / Turquie / Türkei
- 297 United Kingdom / Grande-Bretagne / Grossbritannien

Scandinavia
- 249 Denmark / Danemark / Dänemark
- 269 Finland / Finlande / Finnland
- 271 Norway / Norvège / Norwegen
- 277 Sweden / Suède / Schweden

Portfolio Page Sales Agents

America	Adweek/Art Directors' Index 820 Second Avenue New York, NY 10017 Tel. 212-661 8080 Telex: 177012 adwk ut	Holland	Sedip Mr. P. de Vanssay / Mrs. E. Wibaut Rue Vanderkindere 318 1180 Bruxelles Tel. 2-343 44 99	Norway	TW Marketing Mr. Tor Willy Bjercke Fougstadsgate 22B 0173 Oslo 1 Norway Tel. 02-37 50 80 Fax: 02-37 73 20
Argentina	Documenta srl. Aquiles Ferrario Cordoba 612 entrepiso 1054 Buenos Aires Tel. 1-392 9581 Telex: 9900 bth Fax: 1-311 4385	Hong Kong	David Chan Keng Seng Trading & Co. Loong San Building – Room 103 140-142 Connaught Road Central, Hong Kong Tel. 5-45 50 08 Telex: 64820 kshk hx	Pakistan	M. I. Gaziani Progressive International Agencies P.O. Box 8069 Karachi 29 Tel. 21-43 33 55 Telex: 24786 field pk
Australia	Armadillo Publishers Pty Ltd 205/207 Scotchmer Street Fitzroy North Victoria 3068 Tel. 03-489 95 59 Telex: 30834 displa aa	India	GS Books International Mr. K. S. Ganesh 503 Amit Industrial Estate 61 Dr. S. S. Rao Road, Lalbaug Bombay 400 012 Tel. 413 81 42 Telex: 117 233 6 baas in	Singapore	Mark Tan Page One – The Bookshop Pte Ltd B1-03 & 04, Parkway Parade Marine Parade Road Singapore 1544 Tel. 440 07 11
Austria	Gudrun Tempelmann-Boehr Am Rosenbaum 7 4006 Erkrath Deutschland Tel. 49211-25 32 46 / 39 68 39	Indonesia	Art Graphic Mart – GPS 32 Kwitang Road P.O. Box 4215 Jakarta Tel. 34 42 08 / 36 39 21 Telex: 45366 gps ia	Spain	Editorial Restrepo Felix Boix, 14-1.º E 28036 Madrid Tel. 1-457 33 83 457 45 56
Belgium	Sedip Mr. P. de Vanssay / Mrs. E. Wibaut Rue Vanderkindere 318 1180 Bruxelles Tel. 2-343 44 99	Israel	Avi Kalian Studio 19 Productions Ltd 19a Allenby Street P.O. Box 26177 61 162 Tel Aviv Tel. 03-65 62 70 Telex: 361595 danet il avkan	Sweden	Advision AB Ralph Lidvall Björn Grette Kristinelundsgatan 9 411 37 Göteborg Sweden Tel. 031-203 446 Fax: 031-185 137
Brazil	Talento R. Augusta 2529-1º – Andar 13 CEP 01413 Jardim América São Paulo Tel. 852-1681 Telex: 011 24300	Italy	RotoVision SA 10, rue de l'Arquebuse Case postale 434 1211 Genève 11 Tel. 022-21 21 21 Telex: 421 479 rovi ch Fax: 22/29 91 72	Switzerland	RotoVision SA Christine Rochat 10, rue de l'Arquebuse Case postale 434 1211 Genève 11 Tel. 022-21 21 21 Telex: 421 479 rovi ch Fax: 22/29 91 72 From March 1988: 9, route de Suisse 1295 Mies
Canada	Creative Source Wilcord Publications Ltd 206 Laird Drive – Suite 200 Toronto, Ontario M4G 3W5 Tel. 416-424 4820	Japan	Hideo Kaneko Orion Books Orion Service & Trading Co. Ltd. Papyrus Building 58 Kanda-Jimbocho 1-chome Chiyoda-ku Tokyo 101 Tel. 2-95 4008 Telex: 24408 orion agy	Thailand	Vinai Suttharoj Asia Books Ltd 5, Sukhumvit Soi 61 Sukhumvit Road Bangkok 10110 Tel. 391 2680 / 391 0590 392 8049 / 392 0919 Telex: 21307 asiabks th
Colombia	Ed. Blume de Colombia Ltda Mr. H. Tinjaca Calle 65, No. 16-65 Apartado 51340 Bogotá D.E. Tel. 249 65 35	Luxembourg	Sedip Mr. P. de Vanssay / Mrs. E. Wibaut Rue Vanderkindere 318 1180 Bruxelles Tel. 2-343 44 99	Turkey	Bilimsel Eserler Kollektif Şirketi Sıraselviler Cad. Aylas İş Hanı No. 66 D. 4 Taksim/Istanbul Tel. 1-149 96 33 143 41 73 Telex: 25240 beyg tr
Denmark	Michael Hargreave Christianehøj 50 2860 Søborg Tel. 01-14 14 86 (Office) 69 89 85 (Home)	Malaysia	Johnny Leong Flo Enterprises Sdn. Bhd. 42-A Jalan SS 21/58 Damansara Utama Selangor Tel. 78 77 70 / 78 77 90 Telex: 32958 janas	United Kingdom	RotoVision SA Art Directors' Index 2 St John's Lane London EC1M 4BH Tel. 01-253 5174 Fax: 01-251 8727
Finland	Liikejulkaisut oy/Videc Leena Anttila Fredrikinkatu 27 A 5 PL 398 00121 Helsinki 12 Tel. 90-648 178 Telex: 125 108 videc sf Fax: 90-641 236	Mexico	Marcela Gaxiola Producción MGA S.A. Eugenio Sue 309 1150 México, D.F. Tel. 531 56 08		
France	Stratégies 15, square de Vergennes 75015 Paris Tel. 1-42 50 80 00	New Zealand	Littlejohn's Mr. Peter Cook 170 Victoria Street P.O. Box 2960 Wellington Tel. 852 099 Telex: 3380 northac nz att. Littlejohn's Fax: 04-852 090		
Germany	Gudrun Tempelmann-Boehr Am Rosenbaum 7 4006 Erkrath Tel. 49211-25 32 46 / 39 68 39 Manfred Ostner Kaiserplatz 3 8 München 40 Tel. 089-39 88 58				

INDEX

Australia / Australie / Australien

Golding, Michael 207
41 Cambridge Street
Paddington
Sydney, NSW 2021
Tel. 02-333 949

Taylor, Lynda 206
327 Darebin Road
Thornbury
Melbourne
Victoria 3071
Tel. 03-49 1258

Agent:
The Talent Store
24/37 Albert Road
Melbourne
Victoria 3004
Tel. 03-2443

Belgium / Belgique / Belgien

Maris, Luc 215
Theodoor Van Rijswijck Plaats 7
2000 Antwerpen
Tel. 03-232 41 55

Agent:
Drukkerij & Uitgeverij Roels N.V.
Hogeweg 10-16
2200 Borgerhout
Tel. 03-235 90 96
Telex: 33882 r.print B
Telefax: 03-235 37 62

Trias Creative Team bvba 214
Tulpstraat 4
2008 Antwerpen
Tel. 03-231 75 60

Brazil / Brésil / Brasilien

Briquet Filmes Ltda 162
Av. República do Líbano 150
CEP 04502 São Paulo SP
Tel. 011-887 70 66

Guta & Renner Studio 168
Rua Pacheco Leão 1270 Fds.
CEP 22460 Rio de Janeiro
Tel. 294 80 98
 274 45 05

Messias, Daniel 165
Rua Tupi 821
CEP 01233 São Paulo SP
Tel. 862 97 99

Studio de Comunicação 21 Ltda 166
2799, Augusta Street 21
CEP 01413 São Paulo SP
Tel. 011-853 35 44

T & S Cinema de Animação S/C Ltda 167
Rua 13 de Maio 1016
Bela Vista
CEP 01327 São Paulo SP
Tel. 011-288 73 88

Zweig, Marcio 163
Rua Leandro Dupret 96
CEP 04025 São Paulo SP
Tel. 011-544 29 57

Canada / Canada / Kanada

Cosentino, Carlo 146-147
1168 Sainte-Catherine Street West
Montréal, Québec
H3B 1K1
Tel. (514) 876-1442

Dawson & Associates 153
116 Bedford Road #1
Toronto, Ontario
M5R 2K2
Tel. (416) 926-0730

Illustrated Gallery, Inc., The 154
Designers Walk, 326 Davenport Road
Toronto, Ontario
M5R 1K6
Tel. (416) 323-0383

Labrie, André 148
375B, rue Saint-Laurent
Saint-Romuald côte Levis, Québec
G6V 3W6
Tél. (418) 839-5090

Lafrenière, Anik 149
4060, boulevard Saint-Laurent #102
Montréal, Québec
H2W 1W9
Tel. (514) 286-9619

Leopold, Susan 155
2100 Bathurst Street #403
Toronto, Ontario
M5N 2P2
Tel. (416) 782-0947

Madrick, David Studios 160
10 Savarin Street
Scarborough, Ontario
M1J 1Z8
Tel. (416) 266-0159

Messier, Richard 150
5322 Saint-Urbain
Montréal, Québec
H2T 2W9
Tel. (514) 277-8624

Milne, Jonathan 156-157
17 Trinity Mews, 465 King Street East
Toronto, Ontario
M5A 1L6
Tel. (416) 366-5161

Paper Chameleon 158-159
361 Dundas Street, 3rd Floor
London, Ontario
N6B 1V5
Tel. (519) 672-2538

Studio Catalpa, Inc. 151
1260, rue University #103
Montréal, Québec
H3B 3B9
Tel. (514) 866-7484

**Studio de la Montagne
 Communication Visuelle, Inc.** 152
2105, de la Montagne #300
Montréal, Québec
H3G 1Z8
Tel. (514) 288-7414

INDEX

Denmark / Danemark / Dänemark

Aardestrup, Henning 251
Asåvej 21
9220 Aalborg Ø
Tel. 08-15 79 10

Beierholm, Lars 250
Puggaardsgade 10 st. tv.
1573 Copenhagen V
Tel. 01-12 88 77

Blond, Jes 252
St. St. Blichersgade 23
8000 Århus C
Tel. 06-19 54 95
Agent:
Motivmaskinen
Hjelmensgade 31B
8000 Århus C
Tel. 06-18 89 99

Brandt, Kjeld 253
Kronprinsensgade 14
1114 Copenhagen K
Tel. 01-13 22 60
Fax: 01-93 22 70

Christensen, Ole "Flyv" 254
Klokkestøbergade 8
9000 Aalborg
Tel. +45-8-16 80 20

De Korte, Viki 255
Mejerivænget 15
8310 Tranbjerg
Tel. 06-29 19 30

Forup, Lennart 256
Ambra Allé 37
2770 Kastrup
Tel. 01-50 65 51

Frøjlund, Dan 257
Horsebakken 60
2400 Copenhagen NV
Tel. 01-60 06 96

Hedegaard, Jørgen 258
Willemoesgade 9 st.
2100 Copenhagen Ø
Tel. 01-42 42 90

Hummeluhr, Jesper 259
Rosenørns Allé 33, st. tv.
1970 Frederiksberg C
Tel. 01-39 02 63

3-D Illustrations 266
Cut by Søren Thaae
Maglekildevej 16
1853 Copenhagen
Tel. +451-31 24 42

Kirsten + Karsten Koch 260
Skjoldsgade 11
8260 Viby J
Tel. 06-11 40 10

LM-Illustration 262-263
Tuborg Havnevej 58
2900 Hellerup
Tel. 451-20 11 70

Madsen, Carsten 261
Kronprinsessegade 42, st.
1306 Copenhagen K
Tel. 01-13 13 11

Oberoi, T. 267
Oberoi Graphic Communication
Rytterhusene 39
2620 Albertslund
Tel. National 02-62 10 10
Tel. International +45-2-62 10 10

Petagno, Joe 265
Gl. Kongevej 87
1850 Frederiksberg C
Tel. 01-21 56 05

Preston, Fred 264
Mosevej 2
3450 Allerod
Tel. 02-27 18 38

Viby, Robert 268
Lyngskrænten 13
2840 Holte
Tel. 02-80 53 74

INDEX TO ADVERTISER

SPINAT **250**
Puggaardsgade 10 st. tv.
1573 Copenhagen V
Tel. 01-12 88 77

Finland / Finlande / Finnland

Gray, Stewart 270
Infographics Oy
Annankatu 31-33 D 56
00100 Helsinki
Tel. 90-694 90 14

France / France / Frankreich

Baffou, Patrice 227
9, rue de la Californie
37000 Tours
Tél. 47 05 40 05

Collier, Philipp 229
Agent pour la France:
Véronique Dayle
30, avenue du Général Leclerc
92100 Boulogne
Tél. 1-46 05 39 27

Giroud, Annie-France 228
25/27, boulevard Exelmans
75016 Paris
Tél. 1-45 24 61 85

Jacki (Jacques Tosetto) 231
132, rue du Faubourg-Poissonnière
75010 Paris
Tél. 1-48 74 46 95
et Le Château
Rue du Trê
70130 Evry-le-Châtel
Tél. 25 70 54 76

Pattou, Jean 230
34, place du Concert
59800 Lille
Tél. 20 55 77 54

INDEX

Germany / Allemagne / Deutschland

ACM 234
Lohmarer Strasse 28
5210 Troisdorf
Tel. 02241-7 51 13

ApunktMpunkt 248
Horstweg 29
1000 Berlin 19
Tel. 030-321 40 45

Biswanger, Claus D. 243
Fürstenstrasse 9
8000 München 2
Tel. 089-28 21 93

Fröschl, Andreas 245
L8, 13 Postfach 775
6800 Mannheim 1
Tel. 0621-29 13 56

GraphiCom GmbH 242
Hofkamp 87
5600 Wuppertal 1
Tel. 0202-493 63 01
Fax: 0202-493 63 03

Hilbel, Volker 246
Hirmerweg 26
8000 München 60
Tel. 089-87 36 50

Lichthardt, Ulrich 240-241
Hohenzollernstrasse 128
8000 München 40
Tel. 089-30 17 72
Agent:
Lothar Poppensieker
Grillparzerstrasse 44
8000 München 80
Tel. 089-47 95 69

Moos-Drevenstedt, Erika 244
Paul-Gerhardt-Strasse 23
4156 Willich 2 – Anrath
Tel. 02156-38 06

Schüssler, Alfred 236-237
Heidestrasse 146 A
6000 Frankfurt am Main 60
Tel. 069-46 76 88

Stedtler, Lothar 238
Art Director + Illustrator AGD
Hubertushang 5
5063 Overath
Tel. 02206-2664

Studio Becker GmbH 239
Wiesenau 46
6000 Frankfurt/Main 1
Tel. 069-72 16 25
Telex: 4170777 beck d
Fax: 069-72 16 25
Btx: 069-72 17 08

Towndrow, Arthur H. 235
Grafisches Atelier
Bahnweg 35
4970 Bad Oeynhausen
Tel. 05731-2 90 44

Wohlgemuth, Stephan 247
Steinlestrasse 32
6000 Frankfurt 70
Tel. 069-631 38 72

Holland / Hollande / Holland

Boogaard, Ronald van den 222
Korte Leidsedwarsstraat 37 - 4
1017 PW Amsterdam
Tel. 020-26 15 19

Idetif Graphic 218-219
All-round Illustratieburo
Idetif-Graphic bv
Vossendaal 51
Postbus 272
4870 AG Etten-Leur
Tel. 01659-3457
           4697
Fax: 01659-3243

Van Den Oord, Hans 220
Tel. 070-50 39 12
         45 62 69
Agent:
Cart'ell Graphic Creations
Seinpoststraat 70
2586 HC Den Haag
Tel. 070-50 58 77
Fax: 070-50 48 99

Virgo Design 221
Vondelstraat 154
1054 GT Amsterdam
Tel. 020-18 74 20
Fax: 020-18 26 56

Hong Kong / Hongkong / Hong Kong

Fung, Karl 184
Karl Studio
18-D Fu King Yuen
Chi Fu Fa Yuen
Pokfulam
Hong Kong
Tel. 5-50 10 70
Pager: 3-320251/1070

Lui, Michael 185
Michael Lui Illustration
1601, Chit Lee Commercial Building
30-36 Shaukeiwan Road
Hong Kong
Tel. 5-60 93 57

Ma (Shannon Ma), Fu Keung 183
32A, 10/F, Un Chau Street
Sham Shui Po
Kowloon
Hong Kong
Tel. 3- 87 61 51
        3-728 89 63
Pager: 3-7290222 call 2878
Agent:
Accurate Illustration Studio
32A, 4/F, Un Chau Street
Sham Shui Po
Kowloon
Hong Kong
Tel. 3-728 89 63
        3- 87 61 51

Pokan Designs 187
2 Wing Fung Street, West
1/F
Wanchai
Hong Kong
Tel. 5-28 07 35

Yuen, Tai Yung 186
Room 103
Loong San Building
140-142 Connaught Road
Central
Hong Kong
Tel. 5-45 50 08
Telex: 64820 kshk hx

INDEX TO ADVERTISER

KENG SENG TRADING & CO. **188**
Room 103
Loong San Building
140-142 Connaught Road
Central
Hong Kong
Sheung Wan
P.O. Box 33723
Tel. 5-45 50 08
       5-45 88 70
Cable address: KSTANDBOOK
Telex: 64820 kshk hx
Fax: 5-41 40 25

Japan / Japon / Japan

Aiura, Hiroshi 172-173
Paircity Renaissance 123
24-55 Takanawa 4-chome
Minato-ku
Tokyo 108
Tel. 03-441 4958

Hakamada, Kazuo 171
B-203 Sun Heigths Hachimanyama
8-19 Kamitakaido 1-chome
Suginami-ku
Tokyo 168
Tel. 03-329 2156

Illustrators Salmon 174-175
Dai 33 Fujii Building
3-7 Hiragashi
Toyohira-ku
Sapporo 062
Tel. 011-823 8971

Okazaki, Masato 177
Blue Moon Studio
D-106 Senriyama Royal Plaza
4-39 Senriyama Nishi
Suita-shi
Osaka 565
Tel. 06-339 4149
Fax: 06-339 4150

Sakaguchi, Shigeyuki 178
Clark Kent
402 Green Plaza Takatsu
15-18 Nipponbashi 2-chome
Minami-ku
Osaka 542
Tel. 06-643 1431
          644 4438
Fax: 06-644 6059

Togawa, Ikuo 179
Atom
303 Kitatenma Royal Heights
5-3 Tenma 3-chome
Kita-ku
Osaka 530
Tel. 06-354 0628
Fax: 06-358 1985

INDEX

Luxembourg / Luxembourg / Luxemburg

Kreutz, Will 224
Sam's & Cie
Rue Heine 4
1720 Luxembourg
Tél. 352-49 42 42
        49 43 82

Sam's & Cie 224
Rue Heine 4
1720 Luxembourg
Tél. 352-49 42 42
        49 43 82

Malaysia / Malaisie / Malaysia

Jamil, Zainuddin & Hassan, Mohd. 192
Design Unit
Dewan Bahasa Dan Pustaka
50962 Kuala Lumpur
Tel. 03-248 10 11 Ext. 327

Stan Designers/Illustrators 191
199, Persiaran Zaaba
Taman Tun Dr. Ismail
60000 Kuala Lumpur
Tel. 03-718 22 27
      717 29 72
Fax: 03-717 21 07

Taib, Jaafar 193
Creative Enterprise Sdn. Bhd.
11A2, Bangunan Uda
Jalan Pantai Baru
59200 Kuala Lumpur
Tel. 03-657 77 67
      755 43 35

Yusof, Azman 190
Creative Enterprise Sdn. Bhd.
11A2, Bangunan Uda
Jalan Pantai Baru
59200 Kuala Lumpur
Tel. 03-627 17 20
      755 43 35

INDEX TO ADVERTISER

FLO ENTERPRISE SDN. BHD. 194
42-A, Jalan SS 21/58
Damansara Utama
47400 Petaling Jaya
Selangor
Tel. 718 77 70
     718 77 90

New Zealand / Nouvelle-Zélande / Neuseeland

Bennett, Jeremy 203
20 Carolyne Street
Mt. Victoria
P.O. Box 9181
Wellington
Tel. 847 118
    847 136

Fuller, Stephen 201
The Advertising Picture Company Ltd
P.O. Box 973
Wellington
Tel. 04-873 826

IDA 198
The Illustrators and Designers
Association
P.O. Box 47
371 Auckland 1

Mindseye Graphics Ltd 200
10 Roxburgh Street New Market
P.O. Box 37500
Parnell
Auckland
Tel. 09-502 585

Primrose, Craig Steven 199
45 Coldham Crescent
St. Johns Park
Remuera
Auckland 5
Tel. 09-581 332

Reed, Grant 202
P.O. Box 48-141
Blockhouse Bay – Auckland
Tel. 09-545 000

Norway / Norvège / Norwegen

Graff, Rolf 272
Industrigt. 38 B
0357 Oslo 3
Tel. 02-60 95 33

Malvin, M.M. 276
Brochmannsgt. 3
0470 Oslo 4
Tel. 02-55 26 93

Spalder, Frithjof 273
Ymersv. 1
0588 Oslo 5
Tel. 02-22 88 61

Stephansen-Smith, Kristin 274
Box 7652 Skillebekk
0205 Oslo 2
Tel. 02-55 26 93
     37 47 59

Zibell, Volker 275
Grønnegt. 13 B
0350 Oslo 3
Tel. 02-69 89 28

Osterhausgt. 4 B
0183 Oslo 1
Tel. 02-11 18 08

Spain / Espagne / Spanien

Arnas, Vicente 282-283
Calle Puente Larra 31 – 4.º D
28031 Madrid
Tel. 91-778 17 20

Ballesta, Juan 286
Puerto Rico, 11 Bajo D
28016 Madrid
Tel. 91-250 77 51

Borja, Paul 287
Osa Mayor 96 – 2.º D
28031 Madrid
Tel. 91-207 85 66

Diaz Santana, Humberto 284-285
Comandante Zorita, 49 – 1.º "B"
28020 Madrid
Tel. 91-254 50 50

Grupo Rojo 296
Calle Gramíneas, 3
Urbanización La Grajilla
San Sebastian de los Reyes
28009 Madrid
Tel. 91-654 46 49

Mistiano, Mauro 294
Gral. Alvarez de Castro, 43 – Bajo Dcha.
28010 Madrid
Tel. 91-445 07 77

Orestis 288-289
Zabaleta, 43 – 4.º 2
28002 Madrid
Tel. 91-415 37 21

Ramos, Eugenio 290
Plaza Olavide, 5
28010 Madrid
Tel. 91-448 24 04

Riera, Joaquin 292-293
Rosellón, 231 Pral. 2.ª
08008 Barcelona
Tel. 93-217 14 24

Tabernero, Manolo 291
Santa Adela, 17
28033 Madrid
Tel. 91-763 82 92

Travieso, Miguel 295
Plaza de la Cruz 3
47162 Aldeamayor de S. Martín
(Valladolid)
Tel. 983-55 69 51

Sweden / Suède / Schweden

Netzler, Kurt 278-279
Studio 8 AB
Bagartorpsringen 8
Solna – Sweden
Tel. 08-85 70 07
Fax: 08-85 13 08
Ateljen Täby:
Tel. 08-756 51 00

Trägårdh, Richard 280
Agent:
Einar Båge
Vikvägen 16
133 00 Saltsjöbaden
Tel. 08-717 15 24

Thailand / Thaïlande / Thailand

Punnopatham, Chotiwat 196
310/14 Chareonrath Road
Klongsan
Bangkok 10600
Tel. 438 30 08
     438 20 26

Turkey / Turquie / Türkei

Ateş, Metin 211
Bekârbey Sok. No: 16/1
Davutpaşa, Aksaray/İstanbul
Tel. 1-523 89 41

Berktav, Sedat 211
Kuyumcu İrfan Sok. No: 26/2
Nişantaşı/İstanbul
Tel. 1-130 69 80
     140 78 34

Bilir, Fuat 211
Alaca Mescid Cad. hamam Sok.
Çıkmazı, Yeni Okular İşhanı, Kat:1 No:7
Okcular/Bursa
Tel. 241-15009

Çatak, Necdet 211
Altıyol, Çilek Sok, Akyol İşhanı, No:16/1
Kadıköy/İstanbul
Tel. 1-345 45 00

Deniz, İlkin 211
Kayışdağı Cad. Aykın
Ap. No: 141/1 Daire: 10
Kadıköy/İstanbul
Tel. 1-346 03 53

Erman, Ahmet 211
Etemefendi Cad. Değerbilir Sok.
No: 18, Daire: 7
Erenköy/İstanbul
Tel. 1-360 74 26

Özcan, İskender 211
Hızırbey Cad. 2. Bülbül Sok. No: 9/4
Hasanpaşa/İstanbul
Tel. 1-149 96 33

INDEX

United Kingdom
Grande-Bretagne
Grossbritannien

Artists Inc. Ltd   298
15 Stukeley Street
Covent Garden
London WC2B 5LT
Tel. 01-405 0355

Beard, Terry   299
The Old Police House
Devizes Road
Upavon
Pewsey
Wilts SN9 6ED
Tel. 0980-630177
Agent:
Maggie Mundy
216 King Street
London W6 0RA
Tel. 01-741 5862

Chamberlain, John   301
14 Telston Close
Bourne End
Bucks SL8 5TY
Tel. 06285-21941

Harfield, Mark   300
176 Haverstock Hill
London NW3 2AL
Tel. 01-480 5168
         794 4089
New York:
Tel. 718-388 9055

Industrial Art Studio   302
Roger Full/Industrial Art Studio
Consols
St. Ives
Cornwall TR26 2HW
Tel. 0736-797651
Fax: 0736-794291
Agent for Sweden:
Roberts Long & Co. AB
Nya Torg 11
S–243 00 Höör
Tel. 010-46-413-24008

Pinkbarge   306-307
17 De Walden Street
London W1M 7PJ
Tel. 01-486 1053
       935 1906
       935 2417

Tiner, Ron   303
1 Gordon Road
Exeter
Devon EX1 2DH
Tel. 0392-213066

Towns Artworks, Lynn   304-305
92 Kimberley Road
Penylan
Cardiff CF2 5DN
Tel. 0222-498605

Vaughan, Mike   308-309
216 Sheen Lane
East Sheen
London SW14 8LB
Tel. 01-876 9260
Agent:
Pinkbarge
17 De Walden Street
London W1M 7PJ
Tel. 01-486 1053

VENUS Family, The   310
Contact at either:
63 Wimbourne House
Dorset Road
London SW8 1AJ
Tel. 01-582 2633
or:
Whin Brow Cottage
Hood Lane
Cloughton
Nr. Scarborough
N. Yorkshire YO13 0AT
Tel. 0723-87 08 73

Winn, Chris   311
40 Taverham Road
Drayton
Norwich
Norfolk NR8 6RY
Tel. 0603-860532
Fax: 0603-860532

Young Artists   312
2 Greenland Place
London NW1 0AP
Tel. 01-267 9661
Fax: 01-267 9663

United States
Etats-Unis
Vereinigte Staaten

Allen, Julian   40
31 Walker Street
New York, NY 10013
Tel. 212-925 6550

Art Staff, Inc.   97-99
1200 Penobscot Building
Detroit, Michigan 48226
Tel. 313-963 8240
Ben Jaroslaw/Dick Meissner

Artists International   57-60
Michael Brodie
Estate Cottage
7 Dublin Hill Drive
Greenwich, Connecticut 06830
Tel. 203-869 8010
Tel. 212-713 5490

Asbaghi, Zita   63
104-40 Queens Boulevard
#12X
Forest Hills, NY 11375
Tel. 718-275 1995

Baruffi, Andrea   51
341 Hudson Terrace
Piermont, NY 10968
Tel. 914-359 9542

Baseman, Gary   43-45
385 Eigth Street
#3
Brooklyn, NY 11215
Tel. 718-768 3343
Represented in Los Angeles by:
Nancy Heimberg
Tel. 213-933 8660

Biers, Nanette   138
29 16th Avenue
San Francisco, California 94118
Tel. 415-668 6080

Billout, Guy   68
Represented by:
Renard Represents Inc.
501 Fifth Avenue
New York, NY 10017
Tel. 212-490 2450
Telecopier: 212-697 6828

Bloom, Tom   79
Represented by:
Pat Lindgren
41 Union Square
New York, NY 10003
Tel. 212-929 5590

Brazeal, Lee Lee   96
Houston, Texas
Represented in Chicago by:
Joel Harlib & Assoc.
Tel. 312-329 1370
In Dallas:
Art Rep, Inc.
Linda Smith
Tel. 214-521 5156
In Houston:
Ann Dunphy
Tel. 713-660 7205

Brindak, Hermine   28
29 West 15th Street
New York, NY 10011
Tel. 212-255 3729

Brooks, Andrea   84
41 Union Square West
Suite 1228
New York, NY 10003
Tel. 212-645 0644
Tel. 212-924 3085

Carlson, Frederick H.   20
2335 Meadow Drive
Pittsburgh, Pennsylvania 15235
Tel. 412-371 8951

Chang, Andrew   31
5160 Van Kleeck Street
#1D
Elmhurst, NY 11373
Tel. 718-426 1844
Telecopier: 718-457 7992

Chernishov, Anatoly   70
3967 Sedgwick Avenue
#20-F
Bronx, NY 10463
Tel. 212-884 8122

Christman, Michael   132
116 South El Molino #9
Pasadena, California 91101
Tel. 818-793 1358

Christopher, Tom   29
11-51 30th Road
Long Island City, NY 11102
Tel. 718-278 4661
Represented by:
Helio Galleries
122 St. Marks Place
New York, NY 10009
Tel. 212-529 8122
Farnsworth Gallery
2426 Fillmore Street
San Francisco, California 94115
Tel. 415-563 9347

Conge, Bob   17
28 Harper Street
Rochester, NY 14607
Tel. 716-473 0291
Telecopier in studio

Connally, Connie   93
8826 Kingsley
Dallas, Texas 72531
Tel. 214-340 7818
Represented by:
Sandra Freeman
Tel. 214-871 1956

Criss Illustration, Keith W.   123
4329 Piedmont Avenue
Oakland, California 94611
Tel. 415-547 2528

Cronin, Brian   81-83
2233 Ocean Avenue
#A1
Brooklyn, NY 11229
Tel. 718-998 3155

Cruz, Julia / Pop Geometrix   95
413 North Tyler Street
Dallas, Texas 75208
Tel. 214-948 9603
Represented on the West Coast by:
Brad Benedict
Tel. 213-470 4037

Cusano, Steven R.   65
80 Talbot Court
Media, Pennsylvania 19063
Tel. 215-565 8829

Dank, Leonard   74
800 Cox Lane
PO Box 944
Cutchogue, NY 11935
Tel. 212-222 1717
Tel. 516-734 5496

Dorn III, John Alfred   131
John Alfred Dorn III, Inc.
175 Fifth Avenue/Broadway
Suite 2310
New York, NY 10010
Tel. 619-226 1984

Dunaway, Suzanne Shimek   112
10333 Chrysanthemum Lane
Los Angeles, California 90077
Tel. 213-279 2006

INDEX

Dunnick, Regan 30
1345 University Parkway
Sarasota, Florida 33580
Tel. 813-351 1957
Represented in New York by:
Pat Lindgren
Tel. 212-929 5590
Represented in Dallas by:
Debbie Bozeman
Tel. 214-526 3317
Represented in Los Angeles by:
Roger Shank
Tel. 213-392 9908
Represented in Houston by:
Diana Deoreo
Tel. 713-266 9390
Represented in San Francisco by:
Jan Collier
Tel. 415-552 4252

Eagle, Cameron 48
Represented by:
Pat Lindgren
41 Union Square
New York, NY 10003
Tel. 212-929 5590

Ericksen, Marc 117
1045 Sansome Street
Studio 306-1
San Francisco, California 94111
Tel. 415-362 1214
Represented in Los Angeles by:
Chuck DuBow
Tel. 213-938 5177

Erickson, Kerne 144
Mail: PO Box 2175
Mission Viejo, California 92690
Deliver: 26571 Oliva Place
Mission Viejo, California 92692
Tel. 714-364 1141
Telecopier: 714-837 7250
Represented in Los Angeles by:
Michele Morgan
Tel. 714-551 6445

Garland, Michael 26
78 Columbia Avenue
Hartsdale, NY 10530
Tel. 914-946 4536

Giedd, Richard 85
101 Pierce Road
Watertown, Massachusetts 02172
Tel. 617-924 4350

Giraud, Jean "Moebius" 78
STARWATCHER GRAPHICS, INC.
225 Santa Monica Boulevard
Suite 410
Santa Monica, California 90401
Tel. 213-395 5367
Represented by:
David Scroggy
Tel. 619-222 2476

Goldberg, Richard A. 19
368 Congress Street
Fifth Floor
Boston, Massachusetts 02210
Tel. 617-338 6369
Represented in New England by:
Deborah Lipman
506 Windsor Drive
Framingham, Massachusetts 01701
Tel. 617-451 6528
Tel. 617-877 8830

Goode, Harley 71
30 Resina Road
Monsey, NY 10952
Represented by:
Danelle Durden
Tel. 212-621 9747

Goodrich, Carter 24
134 West 87th Street
New York, NY 10024
Tel. 212-787 9184

Gould Graphics 108
800 Trust Building
Grand Rapids, Michigan 49503
Tel. 616-774 0510

Greger, Carol 49
PO Box 6233
Boston, Massachusetts 02209
Tel. 617-783 4353

Grewe, Nilou 89
4 Wakeman Place
PO Box 749
Larchmont, New York 10538
Tel. 914-834 6820
Fax on premises.
Telex: 646 548

Grimmett, Douglass 55
36 East 23rd Street
New York, NY 10010
Tel. 212-777 1099

Hall, Joan 66
155 Bank Street
Studio H945
New York, NY 10014
Tel. 212-243 6059

Hallgren, Gary 16
231 West 29th Street
#805 New York, NY 10001
Tel. 212-947 1054

Harris, Ellen 75
125 Pleasant Street #602
Brookline, Massachusetts 02146
Tel. 617-739 1867

Harris, Jennifer 94
6723 Meadow
Dallas, Texas 75230
Tel. 214-750 4669
Represented by:
Sandra Freeman
Tel. 214-871 1956

Haverfield, Mary 91
5531 Morningside
Dallas, Texas 75206
Tel. 214-824 6889
Represented by:
Sandra Freeman
Tel. 214-871 1956

Hilliard, Fred 126
5425 Crystal Springs NE
Buinbridge Island, Washington 98110
Tel. 206-842 6003
Represented in New York by:
Sam Brody
Tel. 212-758 0640
Represented in Chicago by:
Ken Feldman
Tel. 312-337 0447
Represented in San Francisco by:
Barb Hauser
Tel. 415-530 2648
Represented in Seattle by:
Donna Jorgensen
Tel. 206-284 5080

Hoff, Terry 130
1525 Grand Avenue
Pacifica, California 94044
Tel. 415-359 4081
Represented in San Francisco by:
Freda Scott
Tel. 415-621 2992

Hogan, Jamie 32
10 Dane Street
Boston, Massachusetts 02130
Tel. 617-522 5503

Hong, Min Jae 27
422 East 14th Street
New York, NY 10009
Tel. 212-674 4320

Hunt, Robert 139
107 Crescent Road
San Anselmo, California 94960
Tel. 415-459 6882
Represented in New York by:
Barbara Gordon Assoc.
Tel. 212-686 3514
Represented in San Francisco by:
Jan Collier
Tel. 415-552 4252
Represented in Los Angeles by:
Randy Pate
Tel. 818-985 8181

James, Bill 90
15840 S.W. 79 Court
Miami, Florida 33157
Tel. 305-238 5709

Jetter, Frances 56
390 West End Avenue
New York, NY 10024
Tel. 212-580 3720

Joyner, Eric 119
660 Clipper Street
#213
San Francisco, California 94114
Tel. 415-821 2641

Kelen, Linda 107
Represented by:
Randi Fiat & Associates
612 North Michigan Avenue
Chicago, Illinois 60611
Tel. 312-784 2343

Kimble, David 137
711 South Flower
Burbank, California 91502
Tel. 213-849 1576
Represented by:
John Steinberg Inc.
Tel. 213-471 0232

Kirchoff/Wohlberg, Inc. 31
866 United Nations Plaza
New York, NY 10017
Tel. 212-644 2020
897 Boston Post Road
Madison, Connecticut 06443
Tel. 203-245 7308

Kirkman, Rick 122
PO Box 11816
Phoenix, Arizona 85061
Represented by:
Paul Willard Associates
815 North First Avenue
Suite 3
Phoenix, Arizona 85003
Tel. 602-257 0097

Koester, Michael 127
272 Gresham
Ashland, Oregon 97520
Tel. 503-488 0153
Represented by:
Woody Coleman
Tel. 216-661 4222

Kohler, Keith 92
1105 Highway 98
Mexico Beach, Florida 34210
Tel. 904-648 5140
Telecopier: 904-648 5344
Represented by:
Chris Kohler
1105 Peachtree Street
Atlanta, Georgia 30309
Tel. 404-876 0315

Kupper, Ketti 22
21 Old Stone Road
Darien, Connecticut 06820
Tel. 203-656 0010
Represented in Dallas by:
Sandra Freeman
Tel. 214-871 1956

Levin, Arnie 41
Marion Moskowitz Represents Inc.
342 Madison Avenue
New York, NY 10017
Tel. 212-719 9879

Lindgren & Smith 77
41 Union Square
New York, NY 10003
Tel. 212-929 5590

Livingston, Francis 142
3916 Sacramento Street
San Francisco, California 94118
Tel. 415-668 5868
Represented by:
Freda Scott
Tel. 415-621 2992

Lose, Hal 88
533 W. Hortter Street—Toad Hall
Philadelphia, Pennsylvania 19119
Tel. 215-849 7635

Mahoney, Katherine 38
60 Hurd Road
Belmont, Massachusetts 02178
Tel. 617-489 0406
Represented in
Boston/New England by:
Deborah Lipman
506 Windsor Drive
Framingham, Massachusetts 01701
Tel. 617-877 8830
Tel. 617-451 6528

Marden, Phil 54
126 Cottage Street
Jersey City, New Jersey 07306
Tel. 201-798 5837
Represented in New York by:
David Starr
Tel. 212-254 0321

Mayforth, Hal 21
Represented by:
ELLA
229 Berkeley Street
Suite 54
Boston, Massachusetts 02116
Tel. 617-266 3858

McGinty, Mick 125
9909 Rancho Caballo
Shadow Hills, California 91040
Tel. 818-353 1422
Represented in Los Angeles by:
Randy Pate & Associates Inc./
The Source
PO Box 687
North Hollywood, California 91603
Tel. 818-985 8181

McNamara Associates, Inc. 101-103
1250 Stephenson Highway
Troy, Michigan 48083
Tel. 313-583 9200
Represented by:
James L. Maniere
President/General Manager
1250 Stephenson Highway
Troy, Michigan 48083
Tel. 313-583 9200

Meehan, Jim 52
402 East 65th Street
Apt. 4F
New York, NY 10021
Tel. 212-737 8806
Tel. 518-239 4513

Moss, Geoffrey 42
Marion Moskowitz Represents Inc.
342 Madison Avenue
New York, NY 10017
Tel. 212-719 9879

Nagle, Candace 128
911 Monterey Road
South Pasadena, California 91030
Tel. 818-799 5243

United States
Etats-Unis
Vereinigte Staaten

Najaka, Marlies Merk 23
241 Central Park West
New York, NY 10024
Tel. 212-580 0058

Nemirov, Meredith 80
142 Kent Street
Brooklyn, NY 11222
Tel. 718-389 5972

Neubecker, Robert 76
395 Broadway
Apartment 14C
New York, NY 10013
Tel. 212-219 8435

Newton, Richard 39
Represented by:
Renard Represents Inc.
501 Fifth Avenue
New York, NY 10017
Tel. 212-490 2450
Telecopier: 212-697 6828

Okamoto, Alan H. 124
152 Central Avenue
#2
San Francisco, California 94117
Tel. 415-626 2501

Osaka, Richard 62
14-22 30th Drive
Long Island City, NY 11102
Tel. 718-956 0015

Pantuso, Mike 36
350 East 89th Street
New York, NY 10128
Tel. 212-534 3511
Represented by:
Torpedo Studios
Tel. 212-502 3976

Paraskevas, Michael 72
Represented by:
Pat Lindgren
41 Union Square
New York, NY 10003
Tel. 212-929 5590

Peck Illustration, E. 115
1344 Blue Heron Avenue
Lucadia, California 92024
Tel. 619-272 8147
Represented by:
Richard W. Salzman

Peters, Bob 121
PO Box 7014
Phoenix, Arizona 85011
Represented by:
Paul Willard Associates
815 North First Avenue
Suite 3
Phoenix, Arizona 85003
Tel. 602-257 0097

Piper, Christian 73
PO Box 991
Old Chelsea Station
New York, NY 10011

Pollie, Lissa 106
609 South Leroy Street
Fenton, Michigan 48430
Tel. 313-629 5340
Tel. 313-629 8855

Porfirio, Guy 111
2360 East Broadway
Tucson, Arizona 85719
Tel. 602-323 0518
Represented by:
Jean Grow
Tel. 312-243 8578
In Phoenix by:
Callahan & Associates
Tel. 602-248 0777

Porter, Walter L. 118
4010 West El Camino del Cerro
Tucson, Arizona 85745
Tel. 602-743 9821

Przewodek, Camille 114
4029 23rd Street
San Francisco, California 94114
Tel. 415-826 3238
Represented by:
Susan Fisher
Tel. 415-928 3640

Pyle, Chuck 134
146 10th Avenue
San Francisco, California 94118
Tel. 415-751 8087
Represented by:
Freda Scott
Tel. 415-621 2992
Represented in Los Angeles by:
Pamela Peek
Tel. 213-660 1596

Raglin, Tim 35
138 West 74th Street
New York, NY 10023
Tel. 212-873 0538

Rieser, William 113
419 Via Linda Vista
Redondo Beach, California 90277
Tel. 213-373 4762
Represented in Chicago by:
Randi Fiat
Tel. 312-784 2343
Represented in New York by:
Irmeli Holmberg
Tel. 718-318 0314

Roman Associates, Inc., Helen 86
140 West End Avenue
Suite 9H
New York, NY 10023
Tel. 212-874 7074
Representing:
William Cone
Deborah Ann Hall
Andrea Mistretta
Anna Rich
Yaél

Rosenthal, Marc 69
230 Clinton Street
Brooklyn, NY 11201
Tel. 718-855 3071

Rother, Sue 133
3916 Sacramento Street
San Francisco, California 94118
Tel. 415-387 7578
Tel. 415-821 1736
Represented in New York by:
Barney Kane and Friends
Tel. 212-206 0322

Rudd, M. Gregory 67
3 Overlook Drive
Monroe, Connecticut 06468
Tel. 203-261 4462

Sano, Kazuhiko 116
105 Stadium Avenue
Mill Valley, California 94941
Tel. 415-381 6377

Saunders, Rob 47
368 Congress Street
Fifth Floor
Boston, Massachusetts 02210
Tel. 617-542 6114
Represented in Los Angeles by:
Randy Pate/The Source
Tel. 818-985 8181
In San Francisco by:
Deborah Ayerst
Tel. 415-974 1755

Shields, William S. 120
14 Wilmot Street
San Francisco, California 94115
Tel. 415-346 0376
Represented in San Francisco by:
Jan Collier
166 South Park
San Francisco, California 94107
Tel. 415-552 4252

Soukup, James 104
Route 1
Seward, Nebraska 68434
Tel. 402-643 2339
Represented by:
Kiki Pollard
Dick Crooks
Alexander/Pollard
848 Greenwood Avenue NE
Atlanta, Georgia 30306
Tel. 404-875 1363
Tampa Bay, Florida 33572
Tel. 813-725 4438

Spencer, Joe 140
11201 Valley Spring Lane
North Hollywood, California 91602
Tel. 818-760 0216

Spollen, Chris 18
Moonlight Press (Studio)
362 Cromwell Avenue
Staten Island, NY 10305
Tel. 718-979 9695
Zap Mail transmitter: 718-351-6667

Steele, Robert Gantt 110
14 Wilmot Street
San Francisco, California 94115
Tel. 415-923 0741
Represented by:
Jan Collier
Tel. 415-552 4252

Sullivan, Melinda May 143
834 Moultrie Street
San Francisco, California 94110
Tel. 415-648 2376

Thon, Bud 136
410 View Park Ct.
Mill Valley, California 94941
Tel. 415-397 5080

Thornley, Blair 64
17 Burr Street
Boston, Massachusetts 02130
Tel. 617-524 1808

Turk, Stephen 50
100 Sullivan Street
Apartment 2F
New York, NY 10012
Tel. 212-226 4578
4120 Coldstream Terrace
Tarzana, California 91356
Tel. 818-342 9796
Represented in Dallas by:
Art Rep Inc.
Linda Smith/Linda Ryan
Tel. 214-521 5156
Represented in San Francisco by:
Ann Koeffler
Tel. 415-885 2714

Vaccarello, Paul 105
505 North Lake Shore Drive
Chicago, Illinois 60611
Tel. 312-664 2233

Vella, Raymond 87
345 Main Street
Apartment 7D
White Plains, NY 10601
Tel. 914-997 1424

Vibbert, Carolyn 129
2265 Larkin Street
Suite 3
San Francisco, California 94109
Tel. 415-474 1985
Represented by:
Freda Scott
Tel. 415-621 2992

Voo, Rhonda 109
8800 Venice Boulevard
Los Angeles, California 90034
Tel. 213-839 1532
Telecopier: 213- 836 0167
Represented in Chicago by:
Carolyn Potts & Associates
Tel. 312-935 1707
Represented in San Francisco by:
Ivy Glick
Tel. 415-536 6056
Represented in San Diego by:
David Scroggy
Tel. 619-222 2476
Represented in Dallas by:
Liz McCann
Tel. 214- 871 0353

Walker, Anna V. 61
770 Bronx River Road
#54
Bronxville, NY 10708
Tel. 914-237 3453

Walker, John S.P. 53
47 Jane Street
New York, NY 10014
Tel. 212-242 3435
Represented in the
United Kingdom by:
Peter Hogan
Tel. 01-671 7905

Walker, Ken 100
PO Box 32086
Kansas City, Missouri 64111
Tel. 816-931 7975

Wasson, Cameron 33
4 South Portland Avenue
#3
Brooklyn, NY 11217
Tel. 718-875 8277

Watson Design/Illustration, S.A. 135
234 Corbett Avenue
San Francisco, California 94114-1817
Tel. Studio 415-626 6554
Represented by:
Millicent Chase-Lalanne
Tel. 415-922 9146

Wicks, Ren 141
5455 Wilshire Boulevard
#1212
Los Angeles, California 90036
Associate of Group West Inc.

Yankus, Marc 25
179 Prince Street
New York, NY 10012
Tel. 212-228 6539

Yeager, Alice 37
3157 Rolling Road
Edgewater, Maryland 21037
Tel. 301-261 4239

Zwingler, Randall 46
Wilmington, Delaware
Tel. 302-478 6063
Represented by:
Nanette Hopkins
The a la Carte Solution
PO Box 323
Haverford, Pennsylvania 19041
Tel. 215-649 8589

United States
Etats-Unis
Vereinigte Staaten

ILLUSTRATORS

Allen, Julian 40
Art Staff, Inc. 97-99
Artists International 57-60
Asbaghi, Zita 63
Baruffi, Andrea 51
Baseman, Gary 43-45
Biers, Nanette 138
Billout, Guy 68
Bloom, Tom 79
Brazeal, Lee Lee 96
Brindak, Hermine 28
Brooks, Andrea 84
Carlson, Frederick H. 20
Chang, Andrew 31
Chernishov, Anatoly 70
Christman, Michael 132
Christopher, Tom 29
Conge, Bob 17
Connally, Connie 93
Criss Illustration, Keith W. 123
Cronin, Brian 81-83
Cruz, Julia / Pop Geometrix 95
Cusano, Steven R. 65
Dank, Leonard 74
Dorn III, John Alfred 131
Dunaway, Suzanne Shimek 112
Dunnick, Regan 30
Eagle, Cameron 48
Ericksen, Marc 117
Erickson, Kerne 144
Garland, Michael 26
Giedd, Richard 85
Giraud, Jean "Moebius" 78
Goldberg, Richard A. 19
Goode, Harley 71
Goodrich, Carter 24
Gould Graphics 108
Greger, Carol 49
Grewe, Nilou 89
Grimmett, Douglass 56

Hall, Joan 66
Hallgren, Gary 16
Harris, Ellen 75
Harris, Jennifer 94
Haverfield, Mary 91
Hilliard, Fred 126
Hoff, Terry 130
Hogan, Jamie 32
Hong, Min Jae 27
Hunt, Robert 139
James, Bill 90
Jetter, Frances 56
Joyner, Eric 119
Kelen, Linda 107
Kimble, David 137
Kirchoff/Wohlberb, Inc. 34
Kirkman, Rick 122
Koester, Michael 127
Kohler, Keith 92
Kupper, Ketti 22
Levin, Arnie 41
Lindgren & Smith 77
Livingston, Francis 142
Lose, Hal 88
Mahoney, Katherine 38
Marden, Phil 54
Mayforth, Hal 21
McGinty, Mick 125
McNamara Associates, Inc. 101-103
Meehan, Jim 52
Moss, Geoffrey 42
Nagle, Candace 128
Najaka, Marlies Merk 23
Nemirov, Meredith 80
Neubecker, Robert 76
Newton, Richard 39
Okamoto, Alan H. 124
Osaka, Richard 62
Pantuso, Mike 36
Paraskevas, Michael 72

Peck Illustration, E. 115
Peters, Bob 121
Piper, Christian 73
Pollie, Lissa 106
Porfirio, Guy 111
Porter, Walter L. 118
Przewodek, Camille 114
Pyle, Chuck 134
Raglin, Tim 35
Rieser, William 113
Roman Associates Inc., Helen 86
Rosenthal, Marc 69
Rother, Sue 133
Rudd, M. Gregory 67
Sano, Kazuhiko 116
Saunders, Rob 47
Shields, William S. 120
Soukup, James 104
Spencer, Joe 140
Spollen, Chris 18
Steele, Robert Gantt 110
Sullivan, Melinda May 143
Thon, Bud 136
Thornley, Blair 64
Turk, Stephen 50
Vaccarello, Paul 105
Vella, Raymond 87
Vibbert, Carolyn 129
Voo, Rhonda 109
Walker, Anna V. 61
Walker, John S.P. 53
Walker, Ken 100
Wasson, Cameron 33
Watson Design/Illustration, S.A. 135
Wicks, Ren 141
Yankus, Marc 25
Yeager, Alice 37
Zwingler, Randall 46

Gary Hallgren

231 W. 29th St.
805
New York, NY 10001
Tel. 212-947 1054

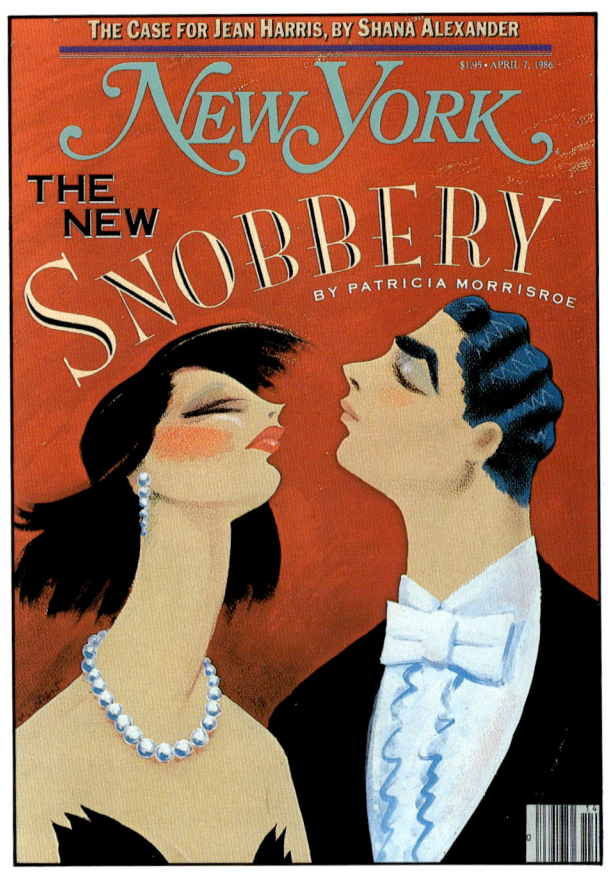

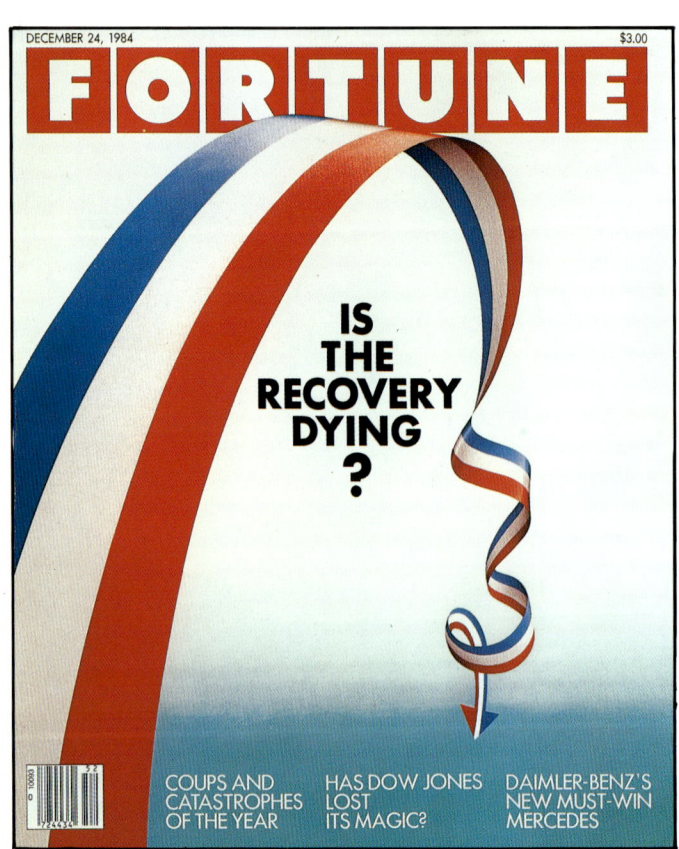

Bob Conge

28 Harper Street
Rochester, NY 14607
Tel. 716-473 0291
Telecopier in studio

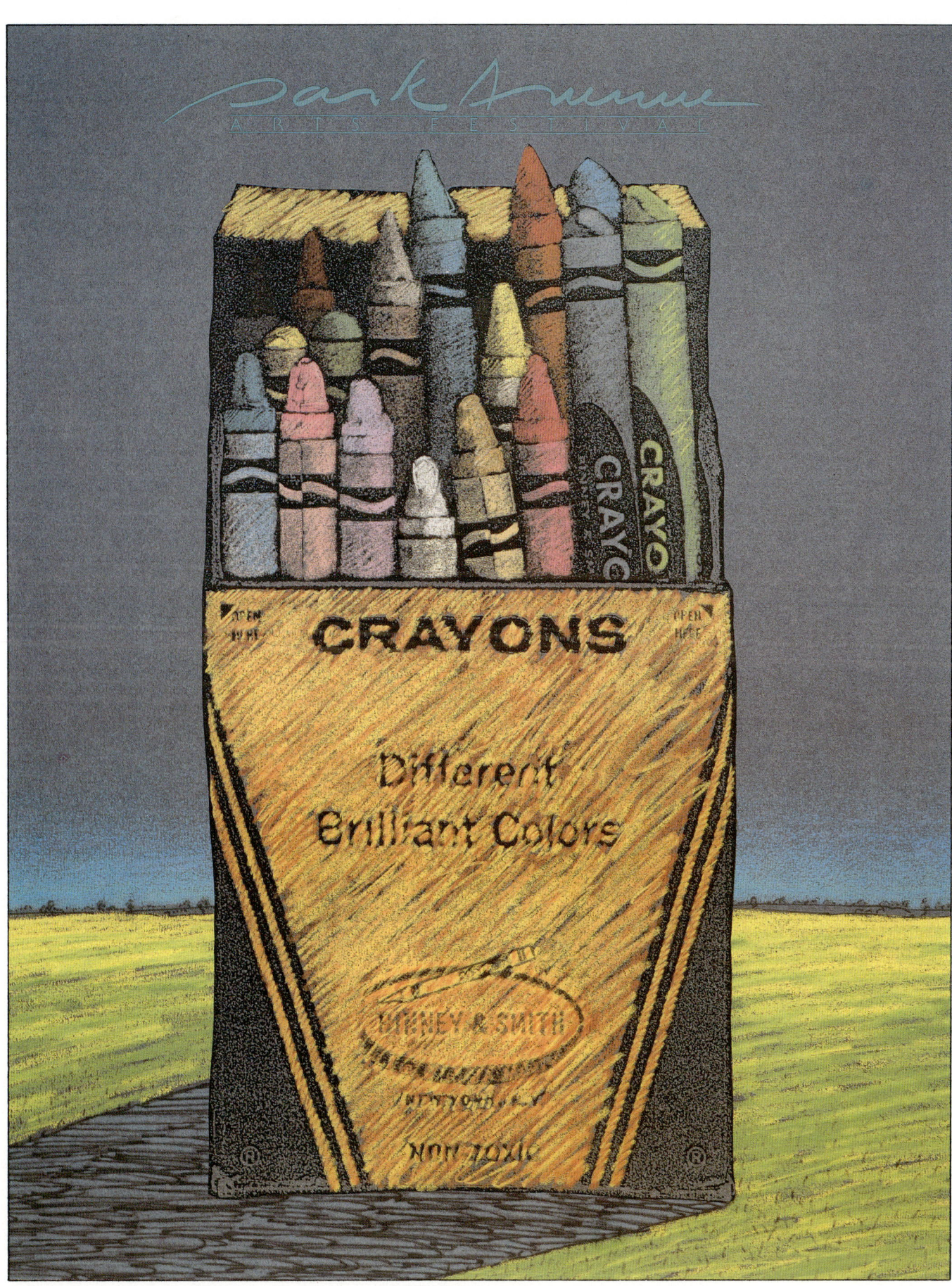

Chris Spollen

Moonlight Press (Studio)
362 Cromwell Avenue
Staten Island, NY 10305
Tel. 718-979 9695
Zap Mail transmitter: 718-351-6667

Richard A. Goldberg

368 Congress Street
Fifth Floor
Boston, Massachusetts 02210
Tel. 617-338 6369

Represented in New England by:
Deborah Lipman
506 Windsor Drive
Framingham, Massachusetts 01701
Tel. 617-451 6528
Tel. 617-877 8830

Frederick H. Carlson

2335 Meadow Drive
Pittsburgh, Pennsylvania 15235
Tel. 412-371 8951

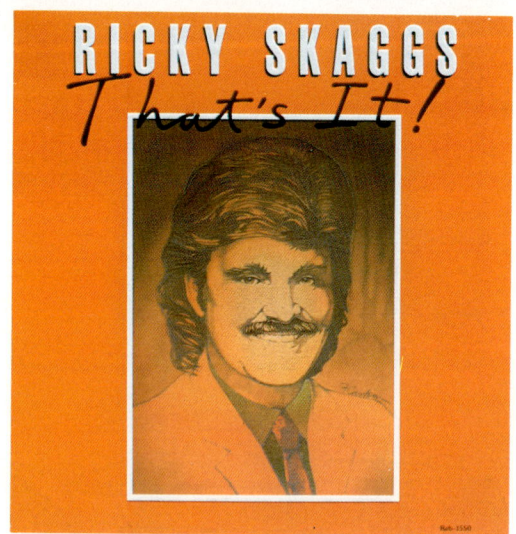

Hal Mayforth

Represented by:
ELLA
229 Berkeley Street
Suite 54
Boston, Massachusetts 02116
Tel. 617-266 3858

Ketti Kupper

21 Old Stone Road
Darien, Connecticut 06820
Tel. 203-656 0010

Represented in Dallas by:
Sandra Freeman
Tel. 214-871 1956

Marlies Merk Najaka

241 Central Park West
New York, NY 10024
Tel. 212-580 0058

Carter Goodrich

134 W. 87th Street
New York, NY 10024
Tel. 212-787 9184

Marc Yankus

179 Prince Street
New York, NY 10012
Tel. 212-228 6539

212-228-6539

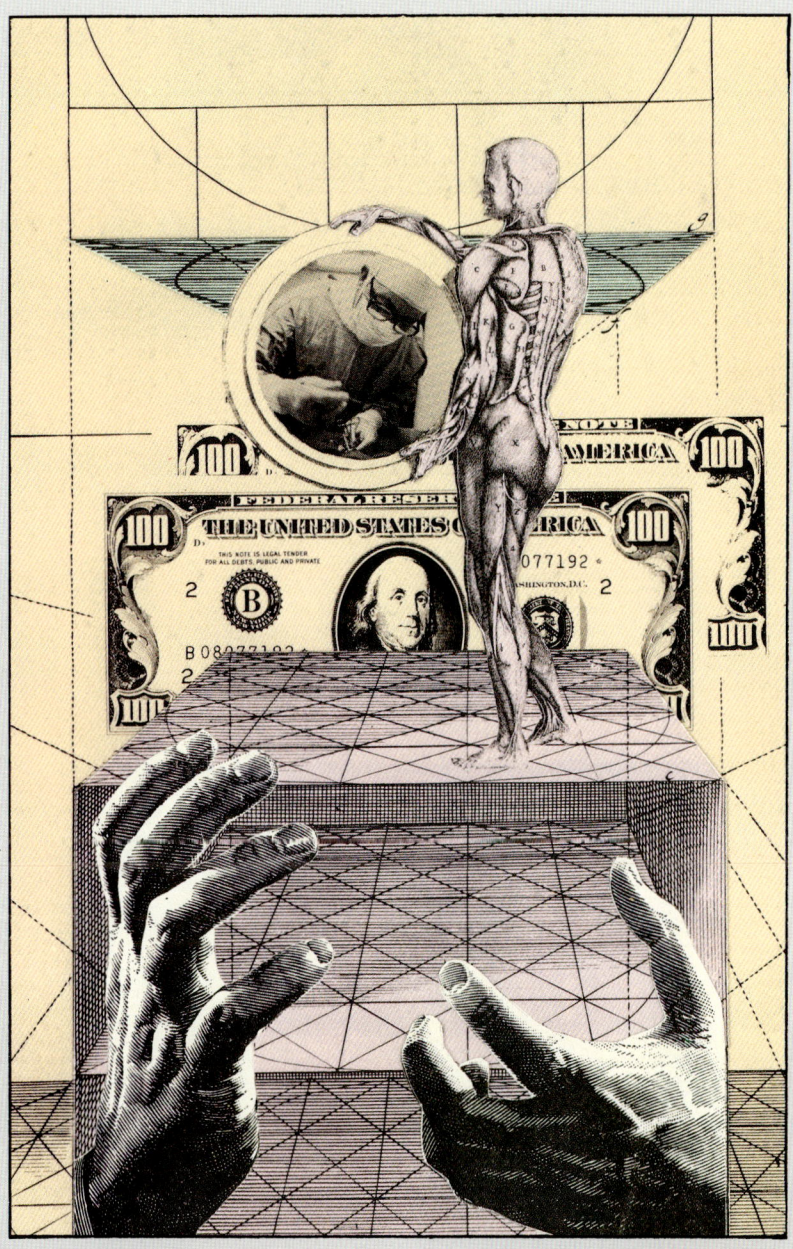

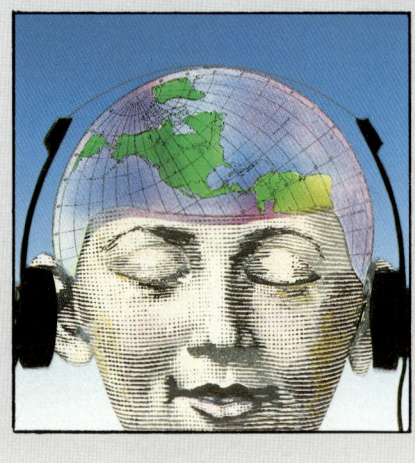

Michael Garland

78 Columbia Avenue
Hartsdale, NY 10530
Tel. 914-946 4536

Min Jae Hong

422 E, 14th Street
New York, NY 10009
Tel. 212-674 4320

Hermine Brindak

29 W, 15th St.
New York, NY 10011
Tel. 212-255 3729

Tom Christopher

11-51 30th Road
Long Island City, NY 11102
Tel. 718-278 4661

Represented by:
Helio Galleries
122 St. Marks Place
New York, NY 10009
Tel. 212-529 8122

Farnsworth Gallery
2426 Fillmore Street
San Francisco, California 94115
Tel. 415-563 9347

Regan Dunnick

1345 University Parkway
Sarasota, Florida 33580
Tel. 813-351 1957

Represented in Dallas by:
Debbie Bozeman
Tel. 214-526 3317

Represented in Houston by:
Diana Deoreo
Tel. 713-266 9390

Represented in New York by:
Pat Lindgren
Tel. 212-929 5590

Represented in Los Angeles by:
Roger Shank
Tel. 213-392 9908

Represented in San Francisco by:
Jan Collier
Tel. 415-552 4252

Andrew Chang

5160 Van Kleeck Street
1D
Elmhurst, NY 11373
Tel. 718-426 1844
Telecopier: 718-457 7992

Jamie Hogan

10 Dane Street
Boston, Massachusetts 02130
Tel. 617-522 5503

Cameron Wasson

4 South Portland Avenue
3
Brooklyn, NY 11217
Tel. 718-875 8277

Kirchoff/Wohlberb, Inc.

866 United Nations Plaza
New York, NY 10017
Tel. 212-644 2020

897 Boston Post Road
Madison, Connecticut 06443
Tel. 203-245 7308

1

2

3

4

5

6

7

8

9

Tim Raglin

138 W. 74th St.
New York, NY 10023
Tel. 212-873 0538

Mike Pantuso

350 E, 89th Street
New York, NY 10128
Tel. 212-534 3511

Represented by:
Torpedo Studios
Tel. 212-502 3976

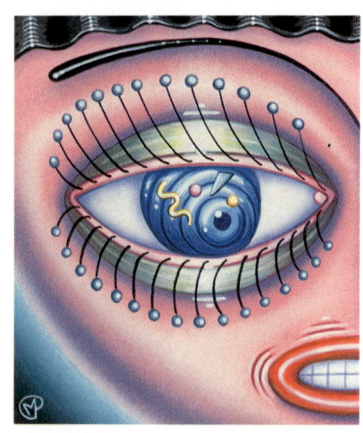

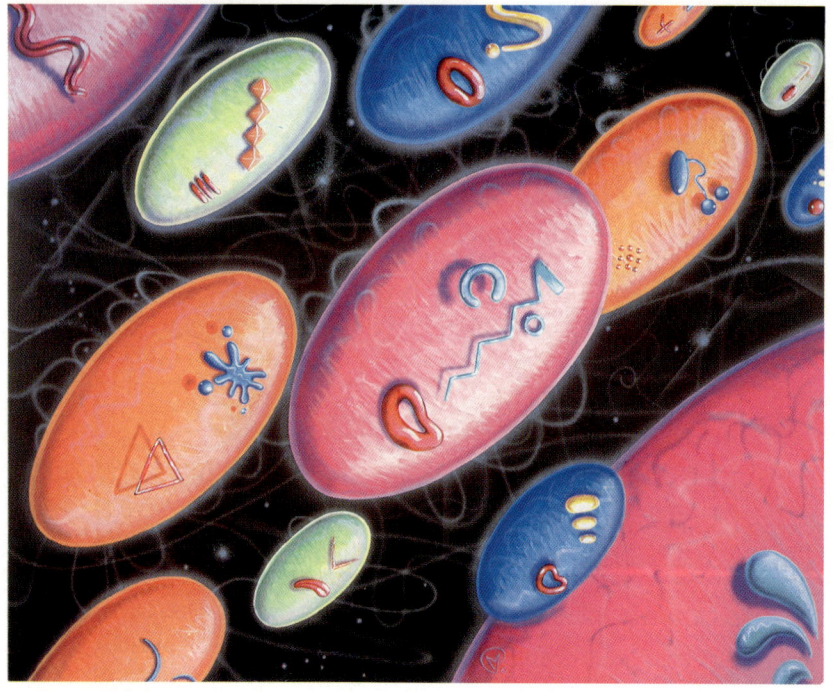
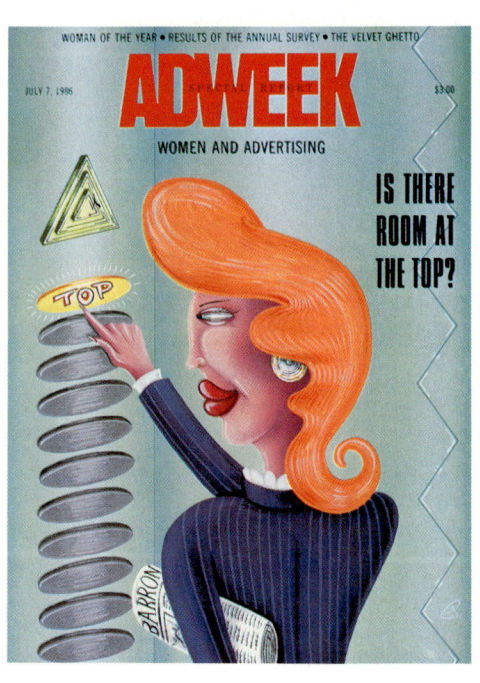

Alice Yeager

3157 Rolling Road
Edgewater, Maryland 21037
Tel. 301-261 4239

Katherine Mahoney

60 Hurd Road
Belmont, Massachusetts 02178
Tel. 617-489 0406

Represented in
Boston/New England by:
Deborah Lipman
506 Windsor Drive
Framingham, Massachusetts 01701
Tel. 617-877 8830
Tel. 617-451 6528

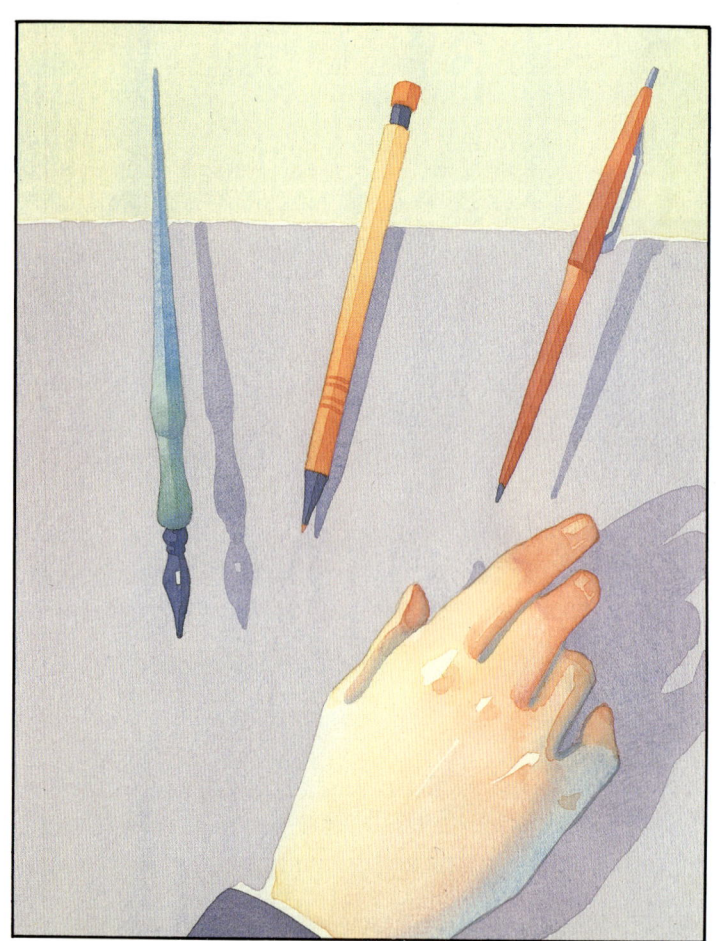

Richard Newton

Represented by:
Renard Represents Inc.
501 Fifth Avenue
New York, NY 10017
Tel. 212-490 2450
Telecopier: 212-697 6828

Julian Allen

31 Walker Street
New York, NY 10013
Tel. 212-925 6550

Arnie Levin

Marion Moskowitz Represents Inc.
342 Madison Avenue
New York, NY 10017
Tel. 212-719 9879

Geoffrey Moss

Marion Moskowitz Represents Inc.
342 Madison Avenue
New York, NY 10017
Tel. 212-719 9879

Gary Baseman

385 Eighth Street
3
Brooklyn, NY 11215
Tel. 718-768 3343

Represented in Los Angeles by:
Nancy Heimberg
Tel. 213-933 8660

Gary Baseman

385 Eighth Street
3
Brooklyn, NY 11215
Tel. 718-768 3343

Represented in Los Angeles by:
Nancy Heimberg
Tel. 213-933 8660

The New York Times
Book Review

June 1, 1986   60¢
© 1986 The New York Times

Robert Baden-Powell: the man who started scouting. Page 7.

Time Out for Summer Reading

Hail Summer! *Overwork, adieu! Welcome, endless days for catching up on the latest best sellers. (What makes a best seller? Anthony Burgess explains, page **3**.) Time to watch a ball game or two. (Harry Stein on the American game and the American dream, page **9**; Dick*

*Francis on why there are so few good sports novels, page **56**.) Time to elevate the spirit (John Russell rounds up art books, page **11**), to make nice dinners (Bryan Miller on cookbooks, page **13**), to flee (travel and guidebooks, pages **14-15**), to rehabilitate the roses*

*(Susan Brownmiller, Lewis Frumkes and Germaine Greer on gardening, pages **30-31**). Whew! It's beginning to sound like work. Well, everybody starts something he can't finish, even famous writers (Symposium, page **38**). Maybe I'll just curl up with one of the year's notable books (cloth, page **39**; paper, page **54**). But first I'll read about new books by Alistair Cooke and Joan Rivers and a first novel by Cathie Pelletier (page **7**).*

Gary Baseman

385 Eighth Street
3
Brooklyn, NY 11215
Tel. 718-768 3343

Represented in Los Angeles by:
Nancy Heimberg
Tel. 213-933 8660

Randall Zwingler

Wilmington, Delaware
Tel. 302-478 6063

Represented by:
Nanette Hopkins
The a la Carte Solution
PO Box 323
Haverford, Pennsylvania 19041
Tel. 215-649 8589

Rob Saunders

368 Congress Street
Fifth Floor
Boston, Massachusetts 02210
Tel. 617-542 6114

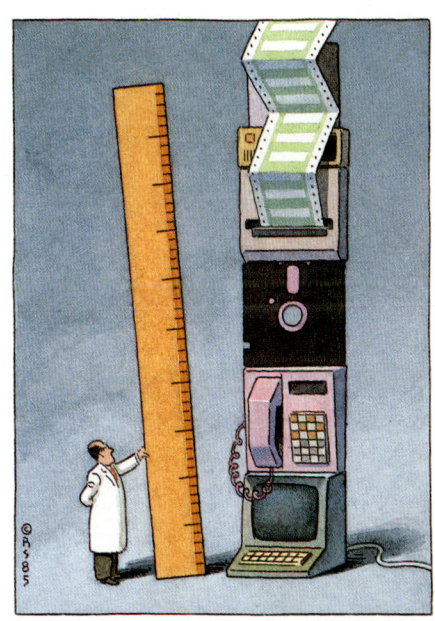

Cameron Eagle

Represented by:
Pat Lindgren
41 Union Square
New York, NY 10003
Tel. 212-929 5590

Mousetrap.

Carol Greger

PO Box 6233
Boston, Massachusetts 02209
Tel. 617-783 4353

Stephen Turk

100 Sullivan Street
Apartment 2F
New York, NY 10012
Tel. 212-226 4578

4120 Coldstream Terrace
Tarzana, California 91356
Tel. 818-342 9796

Represented in Dallas by:
Art Rep Inc.
Linda Smith/Linda Ryan
Tel. 214-521 5156

Represented in San Francisco by:
Ann Koeffler
Tel. 415-885 2714

Andrea Baruffi

341 Hudson Terrace
Piermont, NY 10968
Tel. 914-359 9542

Jim Meehan

402 E. 65th Street
Apt. 4F
New York, NY 10021
Tel. 212-737 8806
Tel. 518-239 4513

John S.P. Walker

47 Jane Street
New York, NY 10014
Tel. 212-242 3435

Represented in the
United Kingdom by:
Peter Hogan
Tel. 01-671 7905

Phil Marden

126 Cottage Street
Jersey City, New Jersey 07306
Tel. 201-798 5837

Represented in New York by:
David Starr
Tel. 212-254 0321

Douglass Grimmett

36 E. 23rd Street
New York, NY 10010
Tel. 212-777 1099

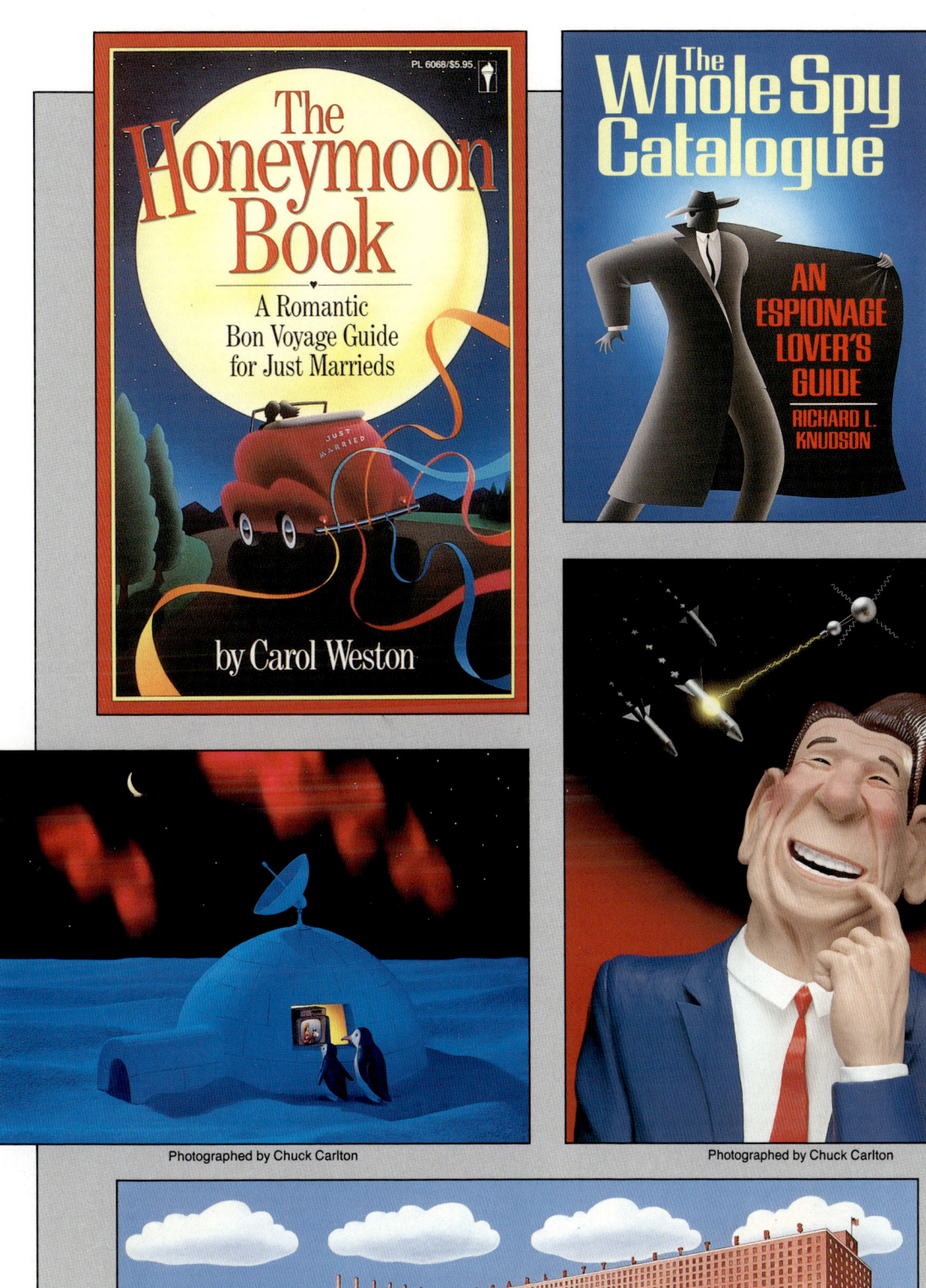

Photographed by Chuck Carlton

Photographed by Chuck Carlton

Frances Jetter

390 West End Avenue
New York, NY 10024
Tel. 212-580 3720

Bookjacket—Franklin Watts

The New York Times

The Franklin Library

Cover—Financial Executives Magazine

Cover—Postgraduate Medicine

Artists International

Michael Brodie
Estate Cottage
7 Dublin Hill Drive
Greenwich, Connecticut 06830
Tel. 203-869 8010
Tel. 212-713 5490

Erik Dzenis

Erik Dzenis

Arthur Singer

© Franklin Mint

Artists International

Michael Brodie
Estate Cottage
7 Dublin Hill Drive
Greenwich, Connecticut 06830
Tel. 203-869 8010
Tel. 212-713 5490

Jeffrey Oh

Jeffrey Oh

Paul Vaccarello

Artists International

Michael Brodie
Estate Cottage
7 Dublin Hill Drive
Greenwich, Connecticut 06830
Tel. 203-869 8010
Tel. 212-713 5490

David Chestnutt

David Chestnutt

Erik Dzenis

Walter Wright

Artists International

Michael Brodie
Estate Cottage
7 Dublin Hill Drive
Greenwich, Connecticut 06830
Tel. 203-869 8010
Tel. 212-713 5490

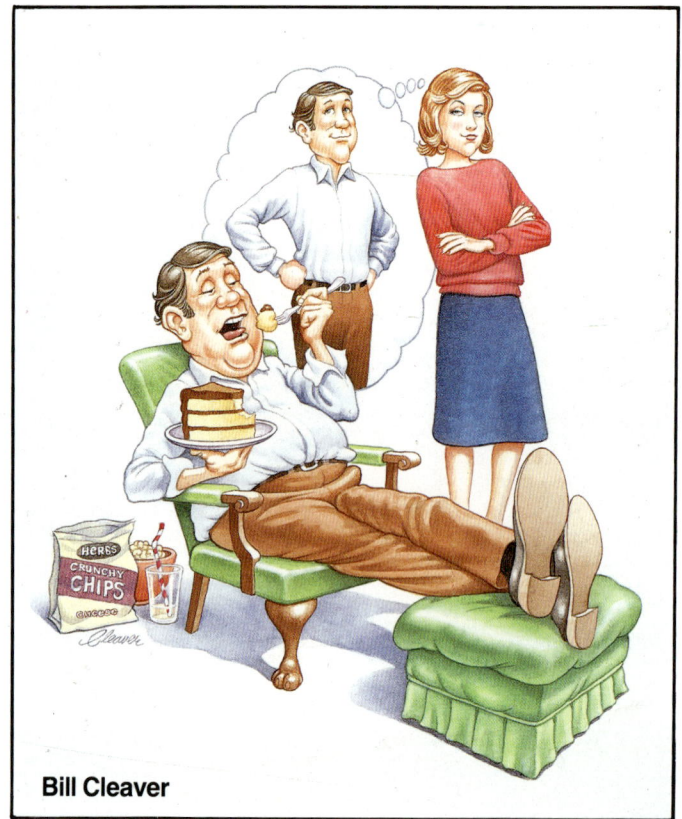

Bill Cleaver

Kathy Spalding

Anna V. Walker

770 Bronx River Road
54
Bronxville, NY 10708
Tel. 914-237 3453

Richard Osaka

14-22 30th Drive
Long Island City, NY 11102
Tel. 718-956 0015

Zita Asbaghi

104-40 Queens Boulevard
12X
Forest Hills, NY 11375
Tel. 718-275 1995

Blair Thornley

17 Burr Street
Boston, Massachusetts 02130
Tel. 617-524 1808

Steven R. Cusano

80 Talbot Court
Media, Pennsylvania 19063
215-565 8829

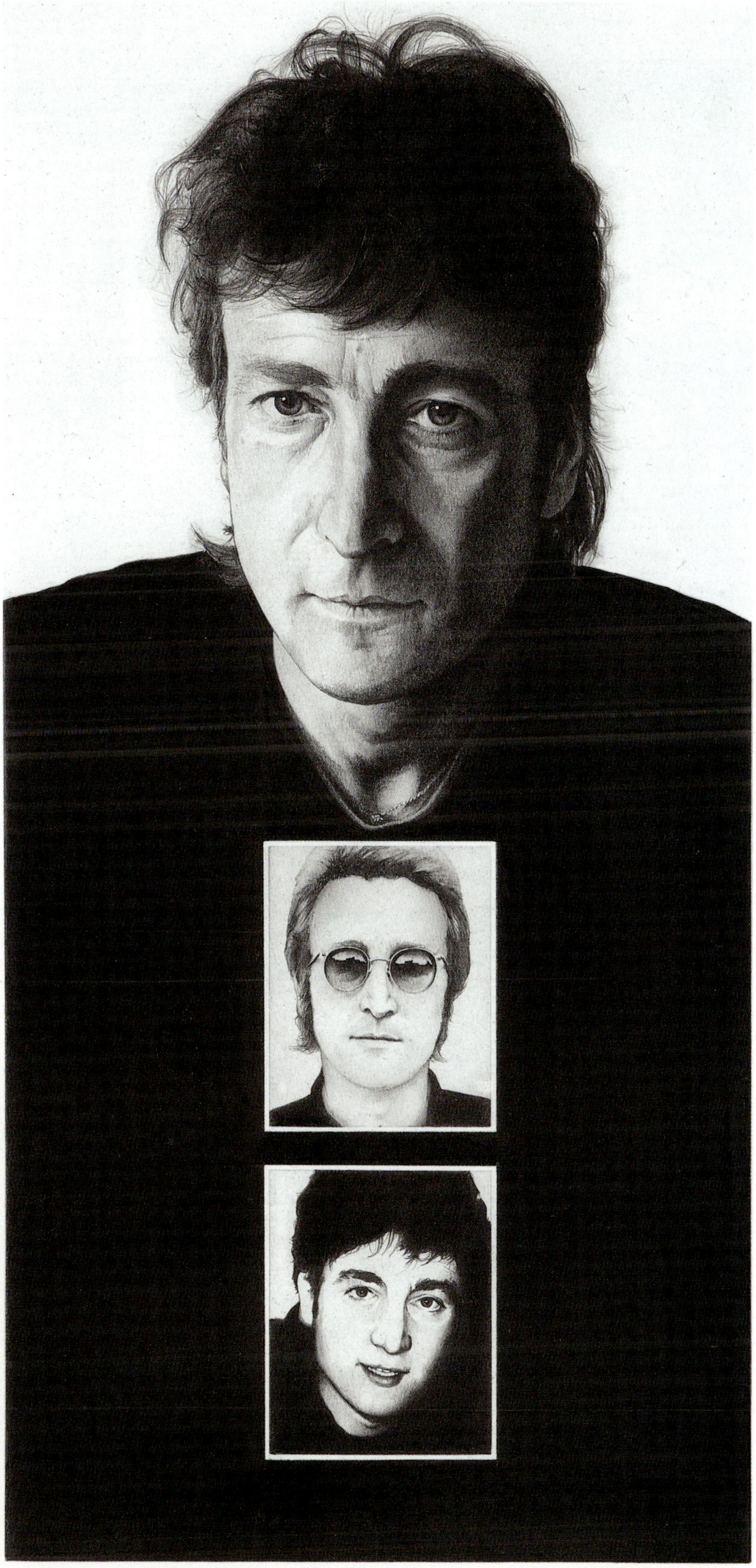

Joan Hall

155 Bank Street
Studio H945
New York, NY 10014
Tel. 212-243 6059

66

M. Gregory Rudd

3 Overlook Drive
Monroe, Connecticut 06468
Tel. 203-261 4462

M. GREGORY RUDD

Guy Billout

Represented by:
Renard Represents Inc.
501 Fifth Avenue
New York, NY 10017
Tel. 212-490 2450
Telecopier: 212-697 6828

Marc Rosenthal

230 Clinton Street
Brooklyn, NY 11201
Tel. 718-855 3071

Anatoly Chernishov

3967 Sedgwick Avenue
20-F
Bronx, NY 10463
Tel. 212-884 8122

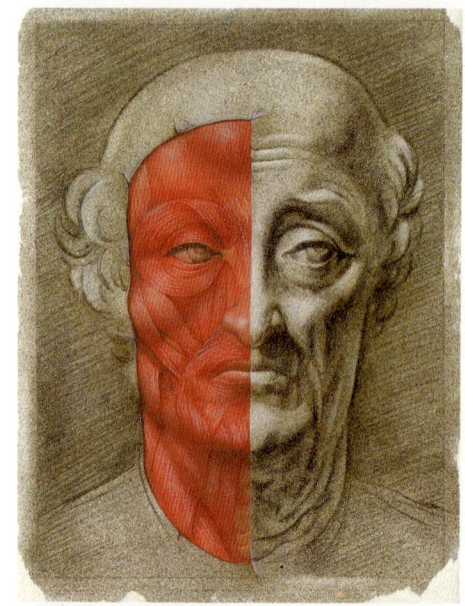
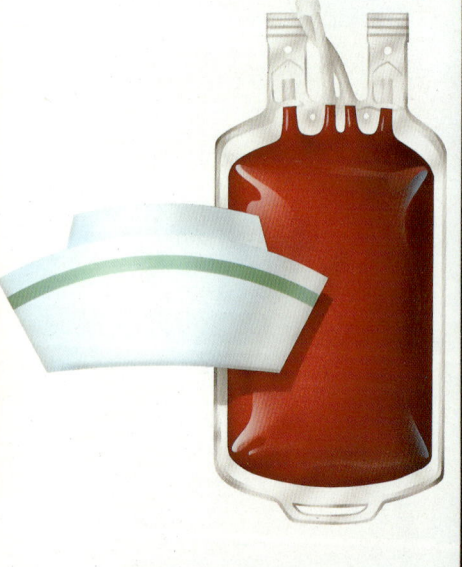
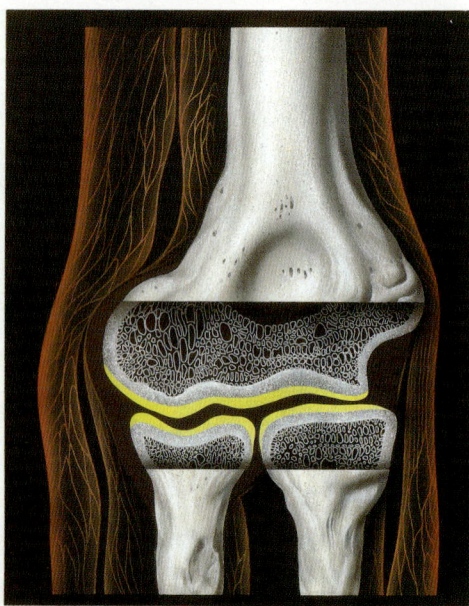

Harley Goode

30 Resina Road
Monsey, NY 10952

Represented by:
Danelle Durden
Tel. 212-621 9747

Michael Paraskevas

Represented by:
Pat Lindgren
41 Union Square
New York, NY 10003
Tel. 212-929 5590

Christian Piper

PO Box 991
Old Chelsea Station
New York, NY 10011

Leonard Dank

800 Cox Lane
PO Box 944
Cutchogue, NY 11935
Tel. 212-222 1717
Tel. 516-734 5496

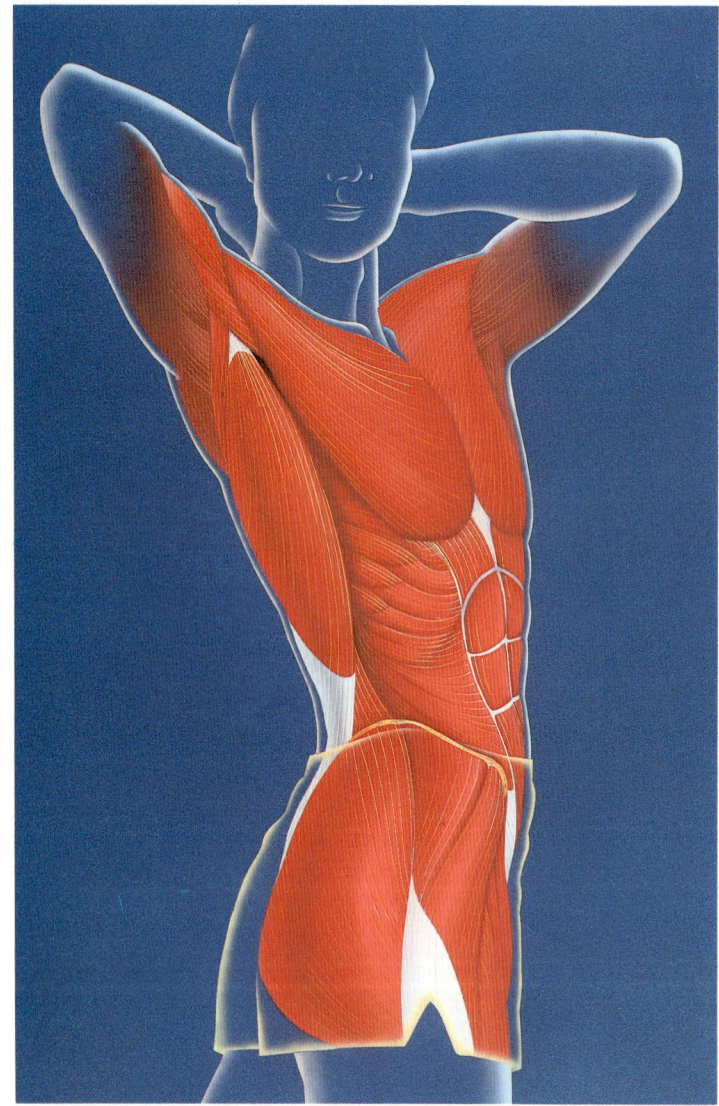
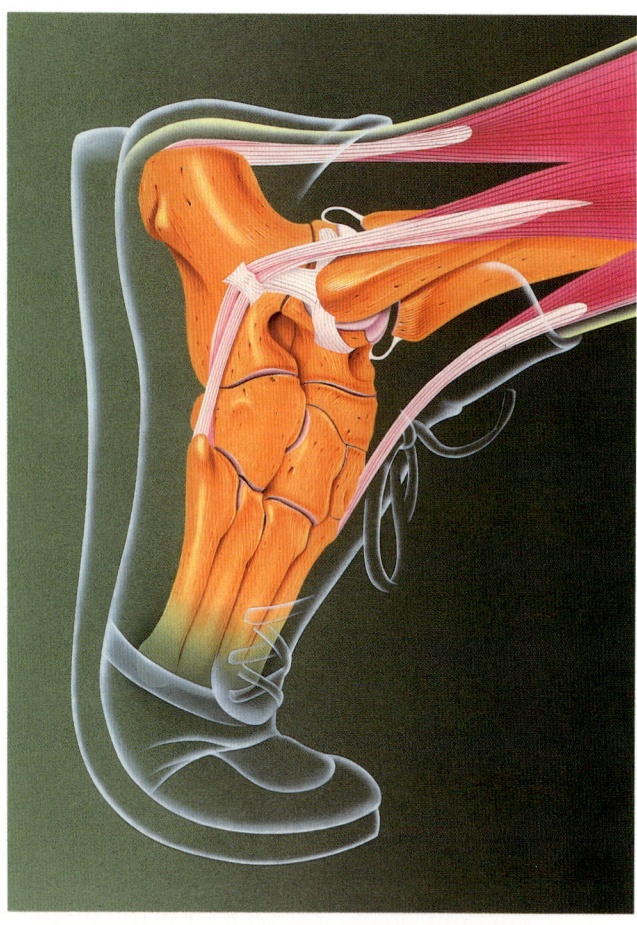
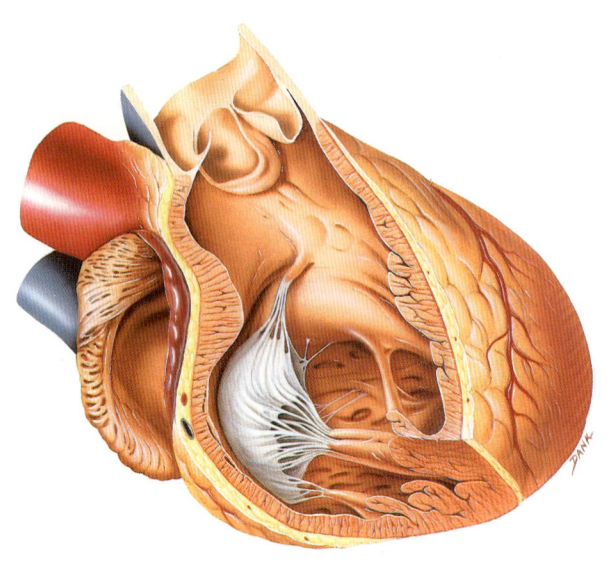
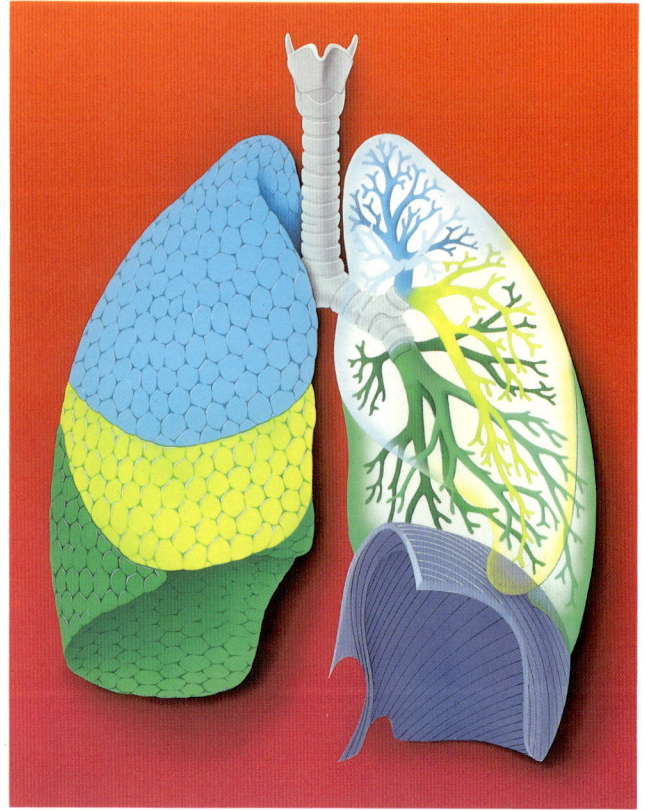

Ellen Harris

125 Pleasant Street - 602
Brookline, Massachusetts 02146
Tel. 617-739 1867

Taking A Chance On Love

Robert Neubecker

395 Broadway
Apartment 14C
New York, NY 10013
Tel. 212-219 8435

PAT LINDGREN

Barbara Banthien

Tom Bloom

Cameron Eagle

Regan Dunnick

Michael Paraskevas

Kathy O'Brien

Six self portraits.

ARTISTS' AGENT 41 UNION SQUARE SUITE 1228 NY, NY 10003 (212) 929-5590

Jean "Moebius" Giraud

STARWATCHER GRAPHICS, INC.
225 Santa Monica Boulevard
Suite 410
Santa Monica, California 90401
Tel. 213-395 5367

Represented by:
David Scroggy
Tel. 619-222 2476

Tom Bloom

Represented by:
Pat Lindgren
41 Union Square
New York, NY 10003
Tel. 212-929 5590

Meredith Nemirov

142 Kent Street
Brooklyn, NY 11222
Tel. 718-389 5972

Brian Cronin

2233 Ocean Avenue
A1
Brooklyn, NY 11229
Tel. 718-998 3155

Brian Cronin

2233 Ocean Avenue
A1
Brooklyn, NY 11229
Tel. 718-998 3155

Brian Cronin

2233 Ocean Avenue
A1
Brooklyn, NY 11229
Tel. 718-998 3155

Andrea Brooks

41 Union Square West
Suite 1228
New York, NY 10003
Tel. 212-645 0644
Tel. 212-924 3085

84

Richard Giedd

101 Pierce Road
Watertown, Massachusetts 02172
Tel. 617-924 4350

Helen Roman Associates Inc.

140 West End Avenue
Suite 9H
New York, NY 10023
Tel. 212-874 7074

Representing:
William Cone
Deborah Ann Hall
Andrea Mistretta
Anna Rich
Yaél

Andrea Mistretta

William Cone

Anna Rich

Deborah Ann Hall

Yaél

Raymond Vella

345 Main Street
Apartment 7D
White Plains, NY 10601
Tel. 914-997 1424

Hal Lose

533 W. Hortter Street—Toad Hall
Philadelphia, Pennsylvania 19119
Tel. 215-849 7635

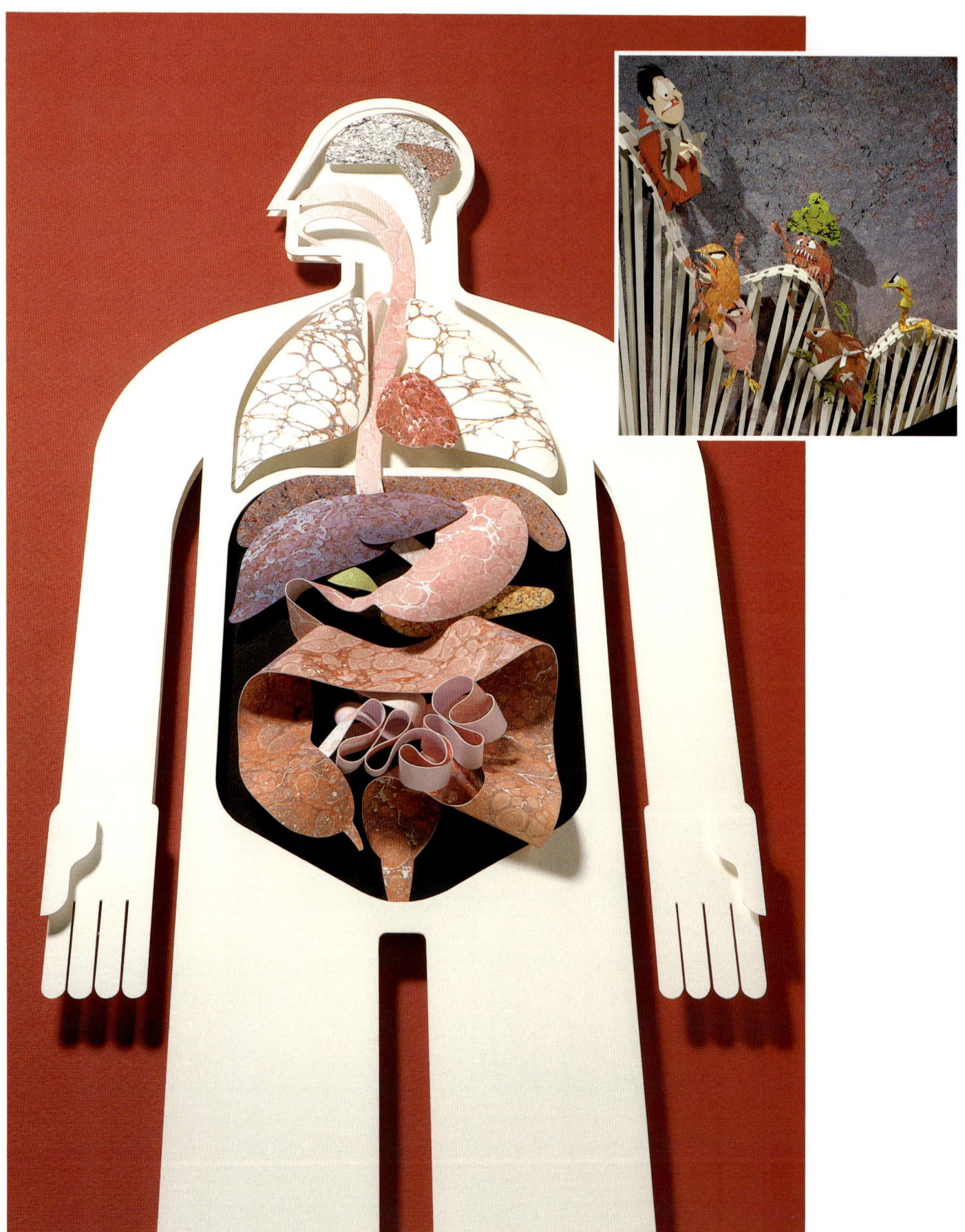

Nilou Grewe

4 Wakeman Place
PO Box 749
Larchmont, New York 10538
Tel. 914-834 6820
Fax on premises.
Telex: 646 548

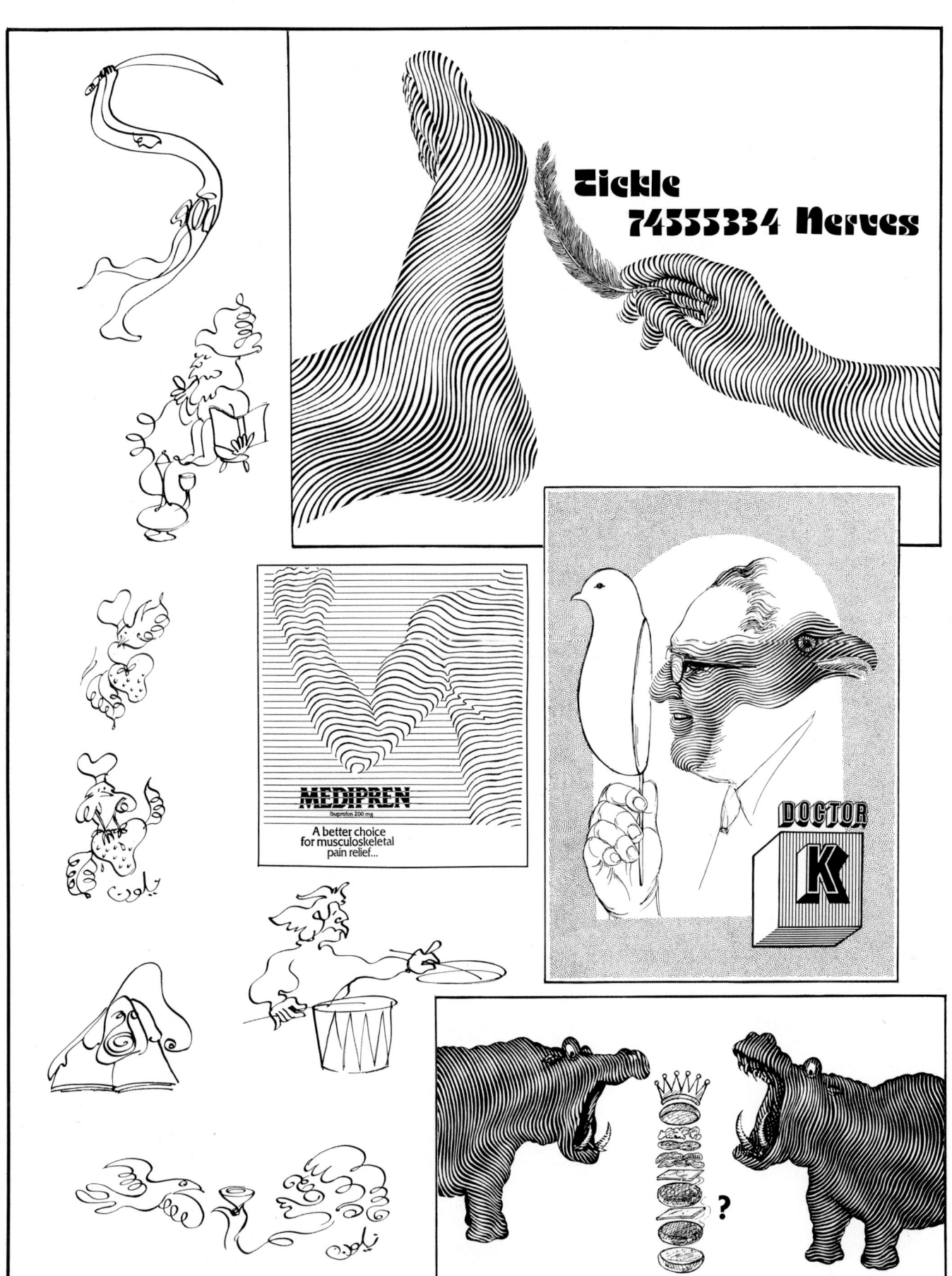

Bill James

15840 S.W. 79 Court
Miami, Florida 33157
Tel. 305-238 5709

Mary Haverfield

5531 Morningside
Dallas, Texas 75206
Tel. 214-824 6889

Represented by:
Sandra Freeman
Tel. 214-871 1956

Keith Kohler

1105 Highway 98
Mexico Beach, Florida 34210
Tel. 904-648 5140
Telecopier: 904-648 5344

Represented by:
Chris Kohler
1105 Peachtree Street
Atlanta, Georgia 30309
Tel. 404-876 0315

Connie Connally

8826 Kingsley
Dallas, Texas 72531
Tel. 214-340 7818

Represented by:
Sandra Freeman
Tel. 214-871 1956

Jennifer Harris

6723 Meadow
Dallas, Texas 75230
Tel. 214-750 4669

Represented by:
Sandra Freeman
Tel. 214-871 1956

Julia Cruz/Pop Geometrix

413 N. Tyler Street
Dallas, Texas 75208
Tel. 214-948 9603

Represented on the West Coast by:
Brad Benedict
Tel. 213-470 4037

Lee Lee Brazeal

Houston, Texas

Represented in Chicago by:
Joel Harlib & Assoc.
Tel. 312-329 1370

In Dallas:
Art Rep, Inc.
Linda Smith
Tel. 214-521 5156

In Houston:
Ann Dunphy
Tel. 713-660 7205

Art Staff, Inc.

1200 Penobscot Building
Detroit, Michigan 48226
Tel. 313-963 8240

Ben Jaroslaw/Dick Meissner

Art Staff, Inc.

1200 Penobscot Building
Detroit, Michigan 48226
Tel. 313-963 8240

Ben Jaroslaw/Dick Meissner

98

Art Staff, Inc.

1200 Penobscot Building
Detroit, Michigan 48226
Tel. 313-963 8240

Ben Jaroslaw/Dick Meissner

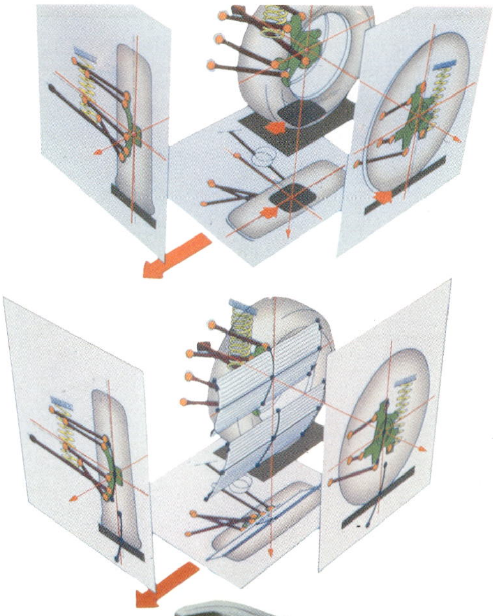

Ken Walker

PO Box 32086
Kansas City, Missouri 64111
Tel. 816-931 7975

McNamara Associates, Inc.

1250 Stephenson Highway
Troy, Michigan 48083
Tel. 313-583 9200

Represented by:
James L. Maniere
President/General Manager
1250 Stephenson Highway
Troy, Michigan 48083
Tel. 313-583 9200

Garth Glazier
Ted Kubit
Don Wieland
Mike Tiderington
Walt Trussell

McNamara Associates, Inc.

1250 Stephenson Highway
Troy, Michigan 48083
Tel. 313-583 9200

Represented by:
James L. Maniere
President/General Manager
1250 Stephenson Highway
Troy, Michigan 48083
Tel. 313-583 9200

McNamara Associates, Inc.

1250 Stephenson Highway
Troy, Michigan 48083
Tel. 313-583 9200

Represented by:
James L. Maniere
President/General Manager
1250 Stephenson Highway
Troy, Michigan 48083
Tel. 313-583 9200

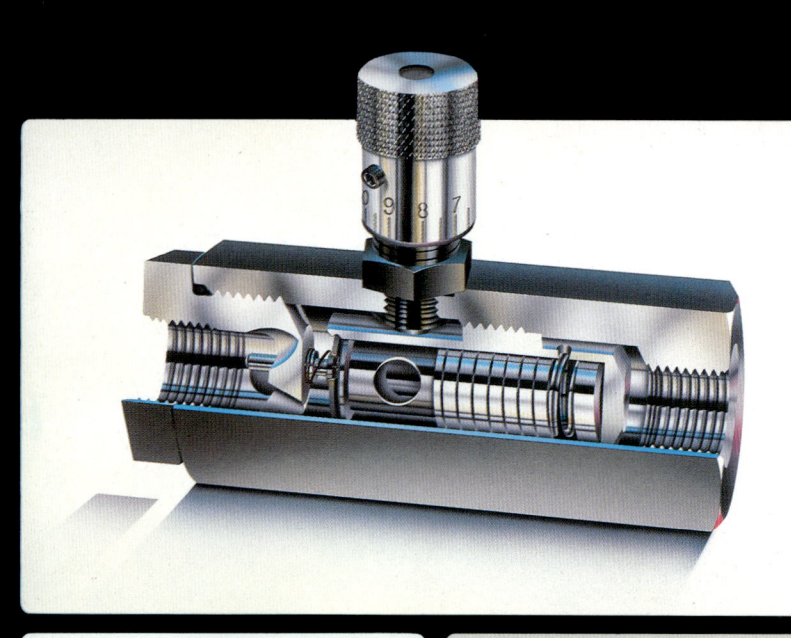

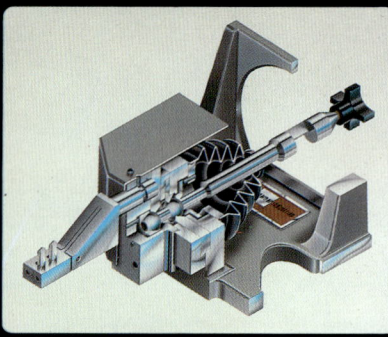
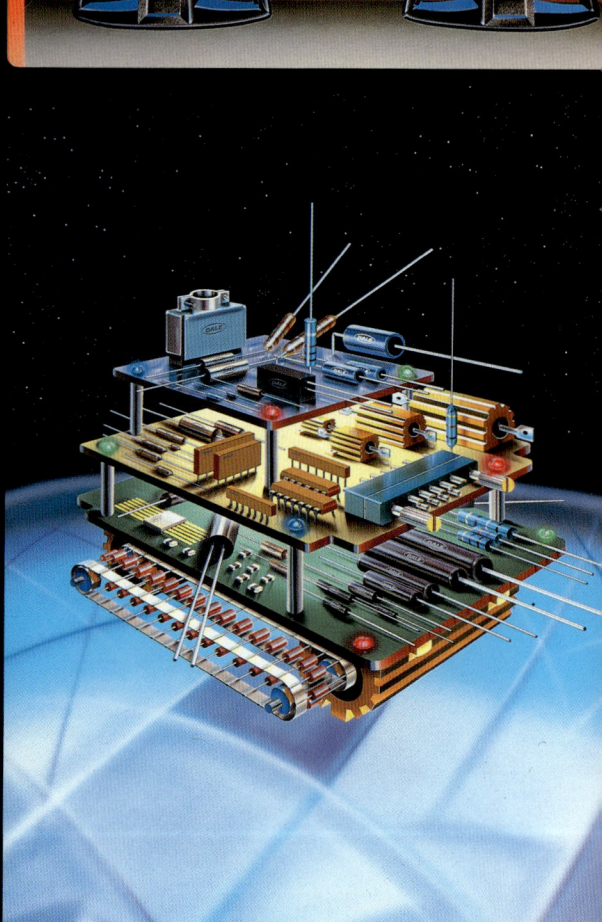

JAMES SOUKUP

REPRESENTED BY

Alexander
P O L L A R D

848 GREENWOOD AVE. N.E.
ATLANTA, GEORGIA 30306
404/875-1363

TAMPA BAY 813/725-4438

Paul Vaccarello

505 N. Lake Shore Drive
Chicago, Illinois 60611
Tel. 312-664 2233

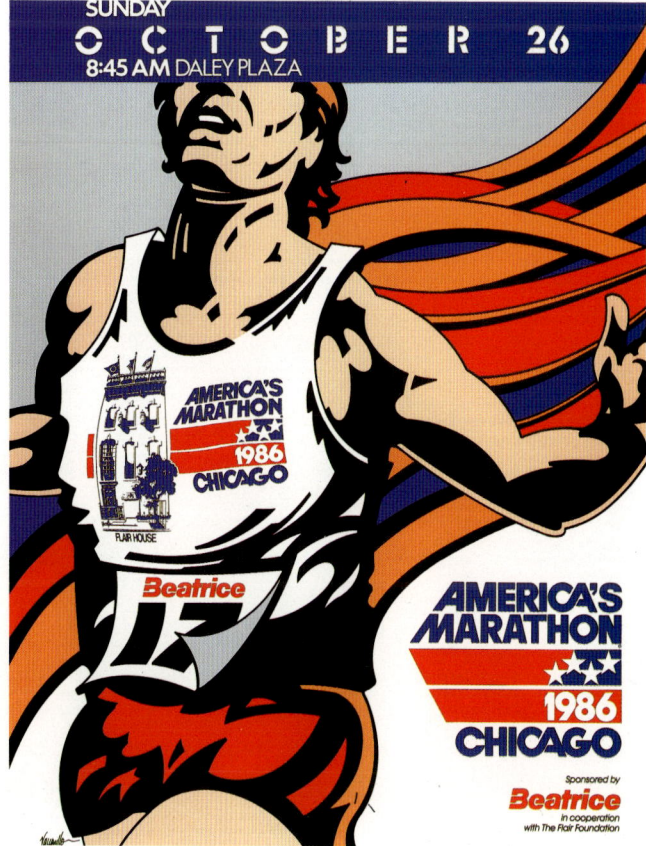

Lissa Pollie

609 S. Leroy Street
Fenton, Michigan 48430
Tel. 313-629 5340
Tel. 313-629 8855

Linda Kelen

Represented by:
Randi Fiat & Associates
612 N. Michigan Avenue
Chicago, Illinois 60611
Tel. 312-784 2343

Gould Graphics

800 Trust Building
Grand Rapids, Michigan 49503
Tel. 616-774 0510

Linda Nelson

Roger Gould

Rhonda Voo

8800 Venice Boulevard
Los Angeles, California 90034
Tel. 213-839 1532
Telecopier: 213-836 0167

Represented in Chicago by:
Carolyn Potts & Associates
Tel. 312-935 1707

Represented in San Francisco by:
Ivy Glick
Tel. 415-536 6056

Represented in San Diego by:
David Scroggy
Tel. 619-222 2476

Represented in Dallas by:
Liz McCann
Tel. 214-871 0353

ADWEEK

Robert Gantt Steele

14 Wilmot Street
San Francisco, California 94115
Tel. 415-923 0741

Represented by:
Jan Collier
Tel. 415-552 4252

Guy Porfirio

2360 E. Broadway
Tucson, Arizona 85719
Tel. 602-323 0518

Represented by:
Jean Grow
Tel. 312-243 8578

In Phoenix by:
Callahan & Associates
Tel. 602-248 0777

Suzanne Shimek Dunaway

10333 Chrysanthemum Lane
Los Angeles, California 90077
Tel. 213-279 2006

William Rieser

419 Via Linda Vista
Redondo Beach, California 90277
Tel. 213-373 4762

Represented in Chicago by:
Randi Fiat
Tel. 312-784 2343

Represented in New York by:
Irmeli Holmberg
Tel. 718-318 0314

Camille Przewodek

4029 23rd Street
San Francisco, California 94114
Tel. 415-826 3238

Represented by:
Susan Fisher
Tel. 415-928 3640

E. Peck Illustration

1344 Blue Heron Avenue
Lucadia, California 92024
Tel. 619-272 8147

Represented by:
Richard W. Salzman

Everett Peck does fine commercial art.

Kazuhiko Sano

105 Stadium Avenue
Mill Valley, California 94941
Tel. 415-381 6377

Represented in Los Angeles by:
Randy Pate/The Source
Tel. 818-985 8181

In San Francisco by:
Deborah Ayerst
Tel. 415-974 1755

Marc Ericksen

1045 Sansome Street
Studio 306-1
San Francisco, California 94111
Tel. 415-362-1214

Represented in Los Angeles by:
Chuck DuBow
Tel. 213-938 5177

© 1986 Darkroom Magazine

© 1986 Intel

© 1986 Communication World Magazine

Walter L. Porter

4010 W. El Camino del Cerro
Tucson, Arizona 85745
Tel. 602-743 9821

Eric Joyner

660 Clipper Street
213
San Francisco, California 94114
Tel. 415-821 2641

William S. Shields

14 Wilmot Street
San Francisco, California 94115
Tel. 415-346 0376

Represented in San Francisco by:
Jan Collier
166 South Park
San Francisco, California 94107
Tel. 415-552 4252

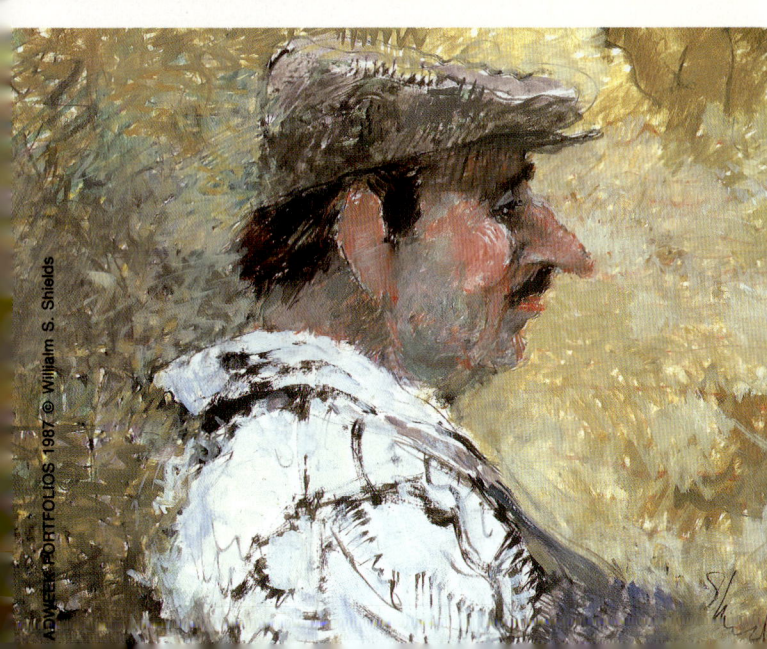

Bob Peters

PO Box 7014
Phoenix, Arizona 85011

Represented by:
Paul Willard Associates
815 N. First Avenue
Suite 3
Phoenix, Arizona 85003
Tel. 602-257 0097

Rick Kirkman

PO Box 11816
Phoenix, Arizona 85061

Represented by:
Paul Willard Associates
815 N. First Avenue
Suite 3
Phoenix, Arizona 85003
Tel. 602-257 0097

Keith W. Criss Illustration

4329 Piedmont Avenue
Oakland, California 94611
Tel. 415-547 2528

Alan H. Okamoto

152 Central Avenue
2
San Francisco, California 94117
Tel. 415-626 2501

ADJA 8 1987 © Alan H. Okamoto

Mick McGinty

9909 Rancho Caballo
Shadow Hills, California 91040
Tel. 818-353 1422

Represented in Los Angeles by:
Randy Pate & Associates Inc./
The Source
PO Box 687
N. Hollywood, California 91603
Tel. 818-985 8181

Fred Hilliard

5425 Crystal Springs NE
Buinbridge Island, Washington 98110
Tel. 206-842 6003

Represented in New York by:
Sam Brody
Tel. 212-758 0640

Represented in Chicago by:
Ken Feldman
Tel. 212-337 0447

Represented in San Francisco by:
Barb Hauser
Tel. 415-530 2648

Represented in Seattle by:
Donna Jorgensen
Tel. 206-284 5080

Michael Koester

272 Gresham
Ashland, Oregon 97520
Tel. 503-488 0153

Represented by:
Woody Coleman
Tel. 216-661 4222

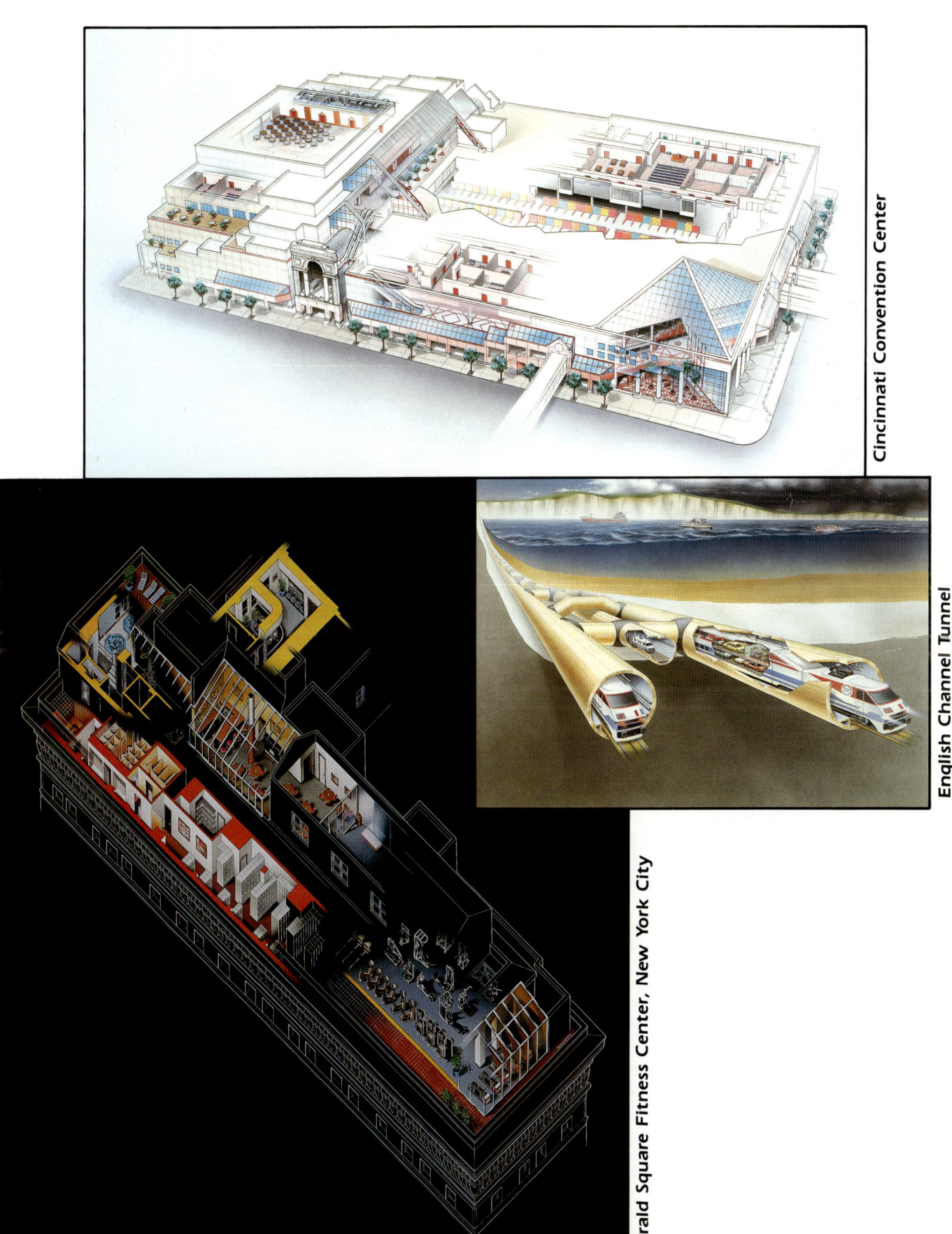

Cincinnati Convention Center

English Channel Tunnel

Herald Square Fitness Center, New York City

Candace Nagle

911 Monterey Road
South Pasadena, California 91030
Tel. 818-799 5243

Carolyn Vibbert

2265 Larkin Street
Suite 3
San Francisco, California 94109
Tel. 415-474 1985

Represented by:
Freda Scott
Tel. 415-621 2992

Terry Hoff

1525 Grand Avenue
Pacifica, California 94044
Tel. 415-359 4081

Represented in San Francisco by:
Freda Scott
Tel. 415-621 2992

130

John Alfred Dorn III

John Alfred Dorn III, Inc.
175 Fifth Avenue/Broadway
Suite 2310
New York, NY 10010
Tel. 619-226 1984

Money magazine

Michael Christman

116 South El Molino # 9
Pasadena, California 91101
Tel. 818-793 1358

Sue Rother

3916 Sacramento Street
San Francisco, California 94118
Tel. 415-387 7578
Tel. 415-821 1736

Represented in New York by:
Barney Kane and Friends
Tel. 212-206 0322

Chuck Pyle

146 10th Avenue
San Francisco, California 94118
Tel. 415-751 8087

Represented by:
Freda Scott
Tel. 415-621 2992

Represented in Los Angeles by:
Pamela Peek
Tel. 213-660 1596

S.A. Watson Design/Illustration

234 Corbett Avenue
San Francisco, California 94114-1817
Tel. Studio 415-626 6554

Represented by:
Millicent Chase-Lalanne
Tel. 415-922 9146

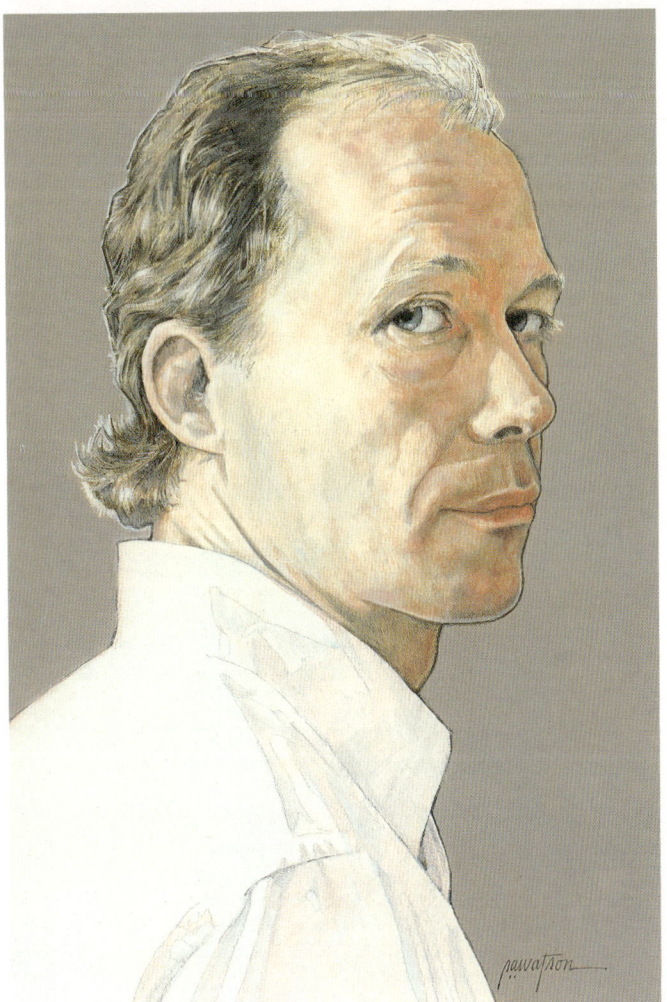

Bud Thon

410 View Park Ct.
Mill Valley, California 94941
Tel. 415-397 5080

David Kimble

711 S. Flower
Burbank California 91502
Tel. 213-849 1576

Represented by:
John Steinberg Inc.
Tel. 213-471 0232

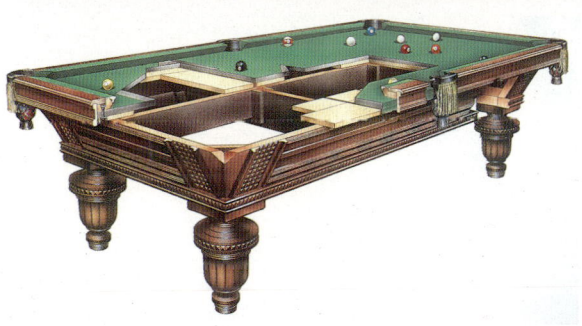

Nanette Biers

29 16th Avenue
San Francisco, California 94118
Tel. 415-668 6080

Robert Hunt

107 Crescent Road
San Anselmo, California 94960
Tel. 415-459 6882

Represented in New York by:
Barbara Gordon Assoc.
Tel. 212-686 3514

Represented in San Francisco by:
Jan Collier
Tel. 415-552-4252

Represented in Los Angeles by:
Randy Pate
Tel. 818-985 8181

Joe Spencer

11201 Valley Spring Lane
N. Hollywood, California 91602
Tel. 818-760 0216

Ren Wicks

5455 Wilshire Boulevard
1212
Los Angeles, California 90036

Associate of Group West Inc.

Francis Livingston

3916 Sacramento Street
San Francisco, California 94118
Tel. 415-668 5868

Represented by:
Freda Scott
Tel. 415-621 2992

Melinda May Sullivan

834 Moultrie Street
San Francisco, California 94110
Tel. 415-648 2376

Kerne Erickson

Mail: PO Box 2175
Mission Viejo, California 92690

Represented in Los Angeles by:
Michele Morgan
Tel. 714-551 6445

Deliver: 26571 Oliva Place
Mission Viejo: California 92692
Tel. 714-364 1141
Telecopier: 714-837 7250

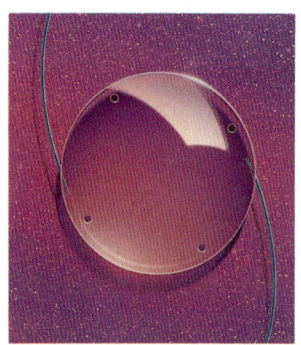
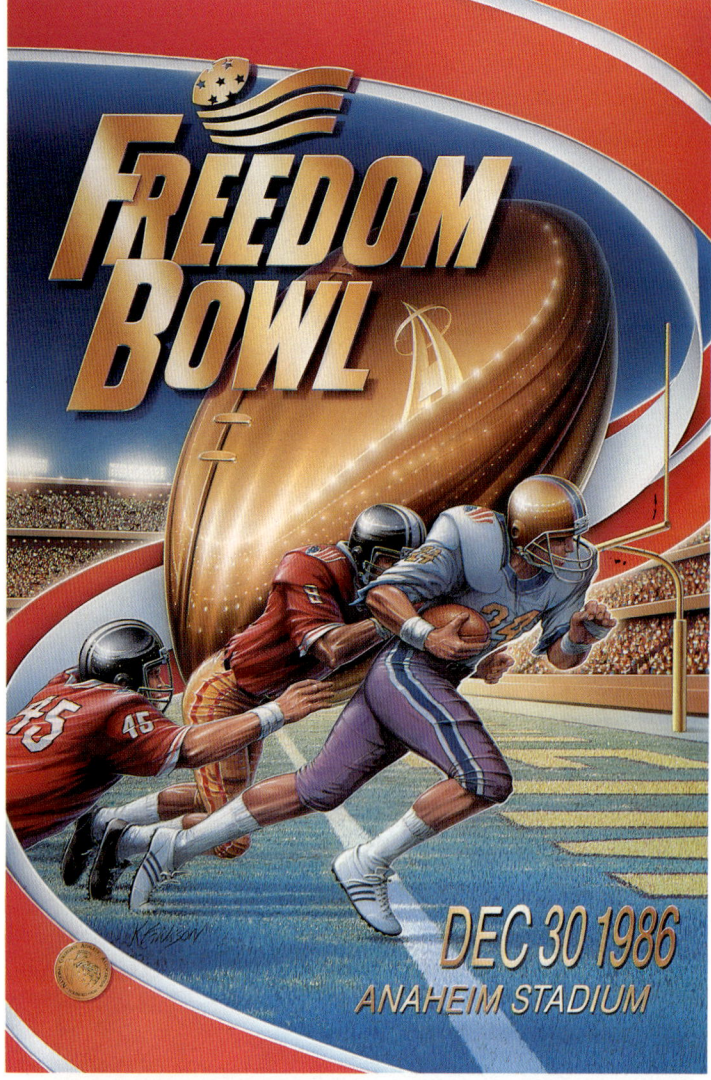

ILLUSTRATORS

Canada
Canada
Kanada

Cosentino, Carlo 146-147
Dawson & Associates 153
Illustrated Gallery, Inc., The 154
Labrie, André 148
Lafrenière, Anik 149
Leopold, Susan 155
Madrick, David Studios 160

Messier, Richard 150
Milne, Jonathan 156-157
Paper Chameleon 158-159
Studio Catalpa, Inc. 151
Studio de la Montagne
 Communication Visuelle, Inc.
 152

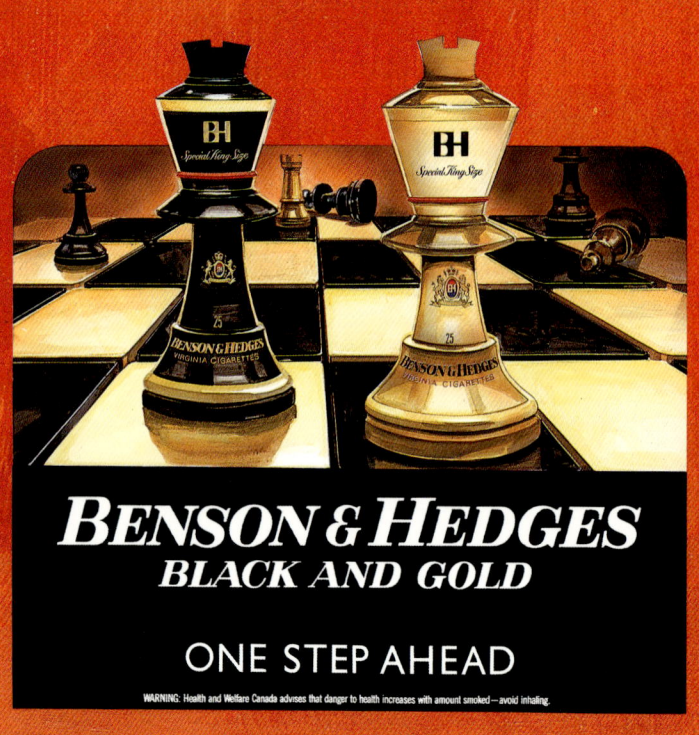

BENSON & HEDGES
BLACK AND GOLD

ONE STEP AHEAD

WARNING: Health and Welfare Canada advises that danger to health increases with amount smoked — avoid inhaling.

Carlo COSENTINO

1168 STE-CATHERINE W. #207, MONTREAL, QC 514·876·1442
CAPIC·ACPIP

ANDRÉ LABRIE

(418) 839 5090
375 B, ST-LAURENT, ST-ROMUALD, QUÉBEC, CANADA   G6V 3W6

ANIK LAFRENIÈRE
4060, BOUL. ST-LAURENT, BUREAU 102, MONTRÉAL, QUÉBEC H2W 1Y9
(514) 286-9619

Richard Messier *illustrateur*

5322, rue St-Urbain, Montréal (Québec) H2T 2W9 Téléphone: (514) 277-8624

Association des illustrateurs et illustratrices du Québec

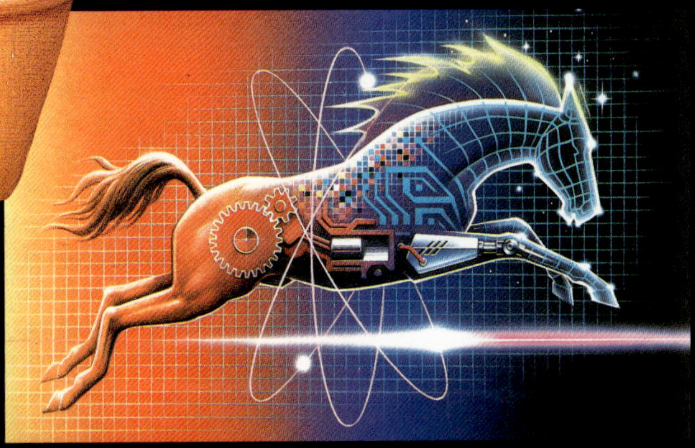

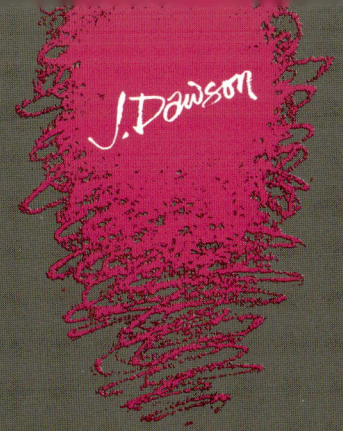

ILLUSTRATION

JOHN DAWSON
116 BEDFORD ROAD, UNIT #1,
TORONTO, ONTARIO, CANADA,
M5R 2K2 (416) 926-0730

C A P I C

**REPRESENTED IN NEW YORK BY:
ALAN LYNCH**
635 MADISON AVE., 9TH FLOOR,
NEW YORK, NY, USA,
10022 (212) 688-1832

TITLE: THE MARKET (UNPUBLISHED)

CANADIAN DOCTOR MAGAZINE, SOUTHAM COMMUNICATIONS, TORONTO

THE NEW ENGLAND MONTHLY, HAYDENVILLE, MASS.

PET CARE REPORT, WHITTLE COMMUNICATIONS, TENN.

HOLT, REINHART & WINSTON OF CANADA LIMITED, TORONTO

[416] 926·0730

A CALL FOR ENTRY

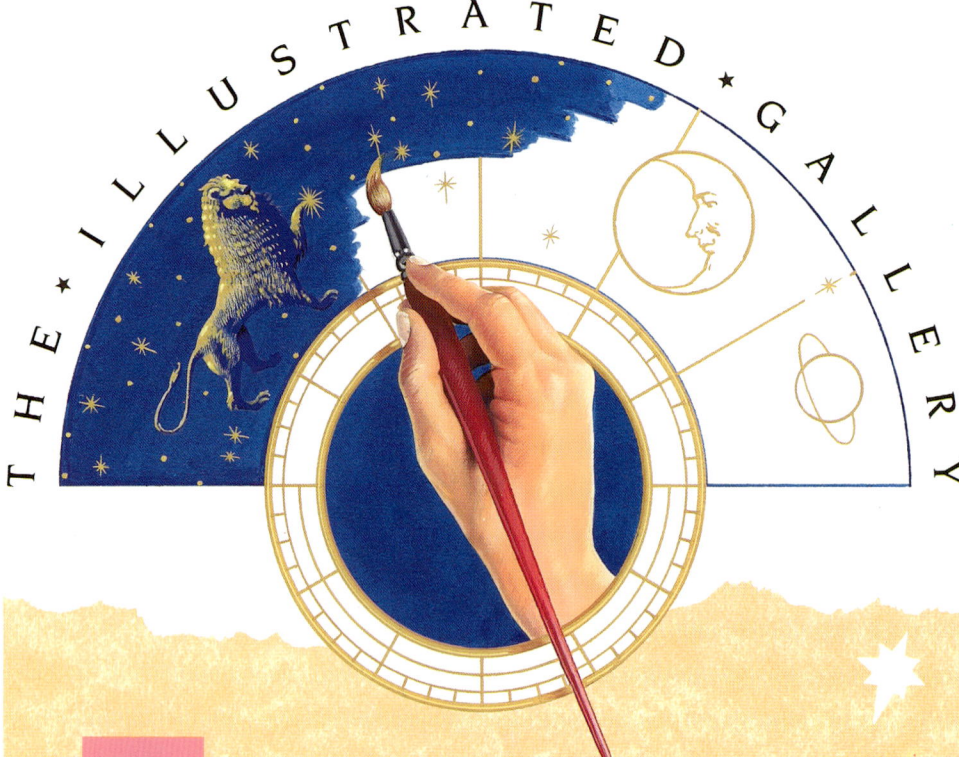

The time has come for the commercial illustrator to be recognized as a fine artist.

In our post-modern era, all forms of art are being re-evaluated and appropriated within the broad classification of fine arts. Contemporary commercial artists, who have for years labored under the bias that their work was something less than art, are now beginning to enjoy the recognition which aligns them to the classical masters of centuries past.

We believe that the public must now be shown the work of the illustrator and be made aware of his or her rightful place in the artistic community. The Illustrated Gallery has been established with this objective in mind.

We encourage all illustrators to retain their original art thereby allowing their work to be sold after publication as the Fine Art that it really is.

The Illustrated Gallery invites you to submit 35 mm slides of your finest commercial work (poster and three-dimensional art also acceptable). All entries must be accompanied by a Curriculum Vitae of the artist and a brief description of the work, including size and medium used. Please enclose a self-addressed stamped envelop to ensure that the slides are returned. Selected works will be accepted on a consignment basis with the exception of certain pieces, which will be acquired by the gallery for our permanent collection.

In addition to illustrative art, The Illustrated Gallery offers the public, much like the studios centuries ago, a comprehensive art service which includes portaiture and murals, as well as design and consulting.

Join us by calling or writing to Ludmilla Temertey at:
Designers Walk, 326 Davenport Road, 2nd Floor
Toronto, Ontario M5R 1K6 (416) 323-0383

Susan Leopold Studios
2100 Bathurst Street
Suite 403
Toronto, Ontario
M5N 2P2

(416) 782-0947
(416) 967-9195

B.F.A., M.A., CAPIC

Detroit
Erinblatt Agency — (313) 559-4100

Illustration of the Grand Hotel, Mackinac Island, Commissioned by Metropolitan Detroit Incorporated

International Papersculpture Ilustrator with Graphic Design and Agency Background. Creative Three Dimensional Illustrations for T.V. and Print. Member CAPIC, The Society of Illustrators N.Y. Association of Illustrators, London.

Jonathan Milne,
Papersculptureworks Inc.,
17 Trinity Mews, 465 King St. East,
Toronto, Ontario, M5A 1L6.
Telephone 416 366-5161

1 Telecom, Canada; 2 Houghton
Brazeau, Canada; 3,5 Licher Bier,
W. Germany; 4 Sports Illustrated, NY;
6 Boro Typographers, NY;
7 Sun Bank, Florida.

RON BRODA
(Paper Sculpture Artist)

Paper Chameleon
361 Dundas Street,
London, Ontario N6B 1V5

(519) 672-2538

Prentice-Hall Canada A/D Gail Ferreira NG-A-Kien

Buntin Reid Paper A/D Gerry Gauthier

Self promotion

Self promotion

1900 Winter Olympic Games Posters for K-Mart and Coca-Cola

Brazil
Brésil
Brasilien

ILLUSTRATORS

Briquet Filmes Ltda   162
Guta & Renner Studio   168
Messias, Daniel   165
Studio de Comunicação 21 Ltda   166
T & S Cinema de Animação S/C Ltda   167
Zweig, Marcio   163

Briquet Filmes Ltda

Av. República do Líbano 150
CEP 04502 São Paulo SP
Tel. 011-887 70 66

Creation of characters, animation, special effects and rotoscopy for a great number of regional and international clients.

Desenvolvimento de personagens, animação, efeitos especiais e rotoscopia para um grande número de clientes regionais e internacionais.

Desenvolvimento de personajes, animación, efectos especiales y rotoscopia por un grande número de clientes regionales y internacionales.

Av. República do Líbano, 150   887 7066   São Paulo, Brasil.

Marcio Zweig

Rua Leandro Dupret 96
CEP 04025 São Paulo SP
Tel. 011-544 29 57

Art Direction, illustration, graphics, photography and airbrush.

Direção de arte, ilustração, artes gráficas, fotografia e aerografia.

Kunstdirektion, Illustration, Grafik, Fotografie und Airbrush Arbeit.

Daniel Messias

Rua Tupi 821
CEP 01233 São Paulo SP – Brazil
Tel. 862 97 99

Working in the field of TV commercials and special effects. Producing over 500 films for the most important agencies: McCann, Standard Ogilvy, JWT, DPZ, Lintas, Young and Rubicam, Almap, etc.

Travaille dans le domaine de la publicité télévisée et des effets spéciaux.
A produit plus de 500 films pour les agences les plus importantes : McCann, Standard Ogilvy, JWT, DPZ, Lintas, Young and Rubicam, Almap, etc.

Arbeitet auf den Gebieten Fernsehwerbung und Spezialeffekte.
Produzent von über 500 Filmen für die wichtigsten Agenturen: McCann, Standard Ogilvy, JWT, DPZ, Lintas, Young and Rubicam, Almap, etc.

Studio de Comunicação 21 Ltda

2799, Augusta Street 21
CEP 01413 São Paulo SP
Brazil
Tel. 011-853 35 44

Directors:
Armando Leal
José Roberto Marcossi

Advertising, promotion, merchandising and photography (original and stock).

Clients:
Empresas Dow, Pronor Petroquímica, Shell Química, Supermercados Barateiro, Goodies Alimentos, Brasval Corretora de Valores, Heublein do Brazil, Tupy Tubos e Conexões, Laboratório Lepetit, Spic Construtora, Spuma Pac, Helfont.

T & S Cinema de Animação S/C Ltda

Rua 13 de Maio 1016
Bela Vista
CEP 01327 São Paulo SP
Tel. 011-288 73 88

Constituída por profissionais com larga experiência nas áreas de produção de comerciais em animação, artes, efeitos especiais e trucagem.

ANIMATION

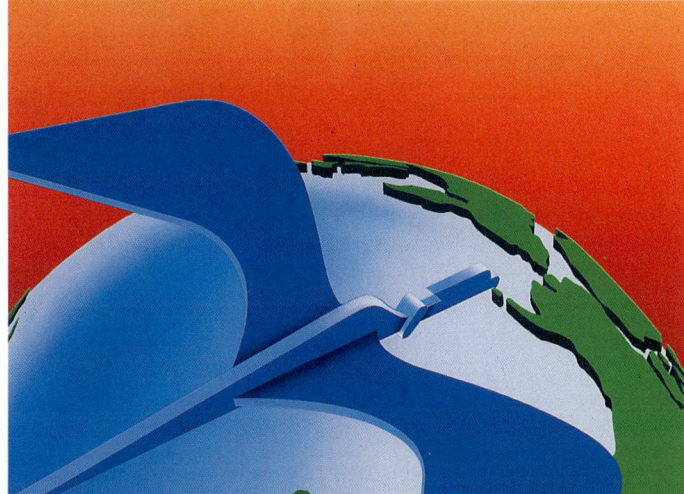
COMPUTER ANIMATION

SPECIAL EFFECTS

ANIMATION

ANIMATION

COMPUTER ANIMATION

Guta & Renner Studio

Rua Pacheco Leão 1270 Fds.
CEP 22460 Rio de Janeiro
Brazil
Tel. 294 80 98
     274 45 05

Realistic and technical illustrations for consumer goods, advertising and packaging. Visual identities for companies, animatics and visual effects. A complete studio service able to produce a wide variety of artworks.

Ilustrações realistas e técnicas para bens de consumo, propaganda e embalagens. Identidade visual para empresas, animatics e efeitos visuais.
Um estudio completo capaz de produzir grande variedade de trabalhos de arte.

Clients advertising agencies:
Alcântara Machado, Artplan, Caio Domingues, DPZ, Denison, Espressão, J.W. Thompson, McCann Erickson, MPM, Pró Varejo, SGB, Standard O&M.
Direct clients:
Rede Globo, Embrafilme, Multifabril, RCA, Gillette, Jornal do Brasil.

ILLUSTRATORS

Japan
Japon
Japan

Aiura, Hiroshi 172-173
Hakamada, Kazuo 171
Illustrators Salmon 174-175
Okazaki, Masato 177
Sakaguchi, Shigeyuki 178
Togawa, Ikuo 179

Kazuo Hakamada

B-203 Sun Heights Hachimanyama
8-19 Kamitakaido 1-chome
Suginami-ku
Tokyo 168
Japan
Tel. 03-329 2156

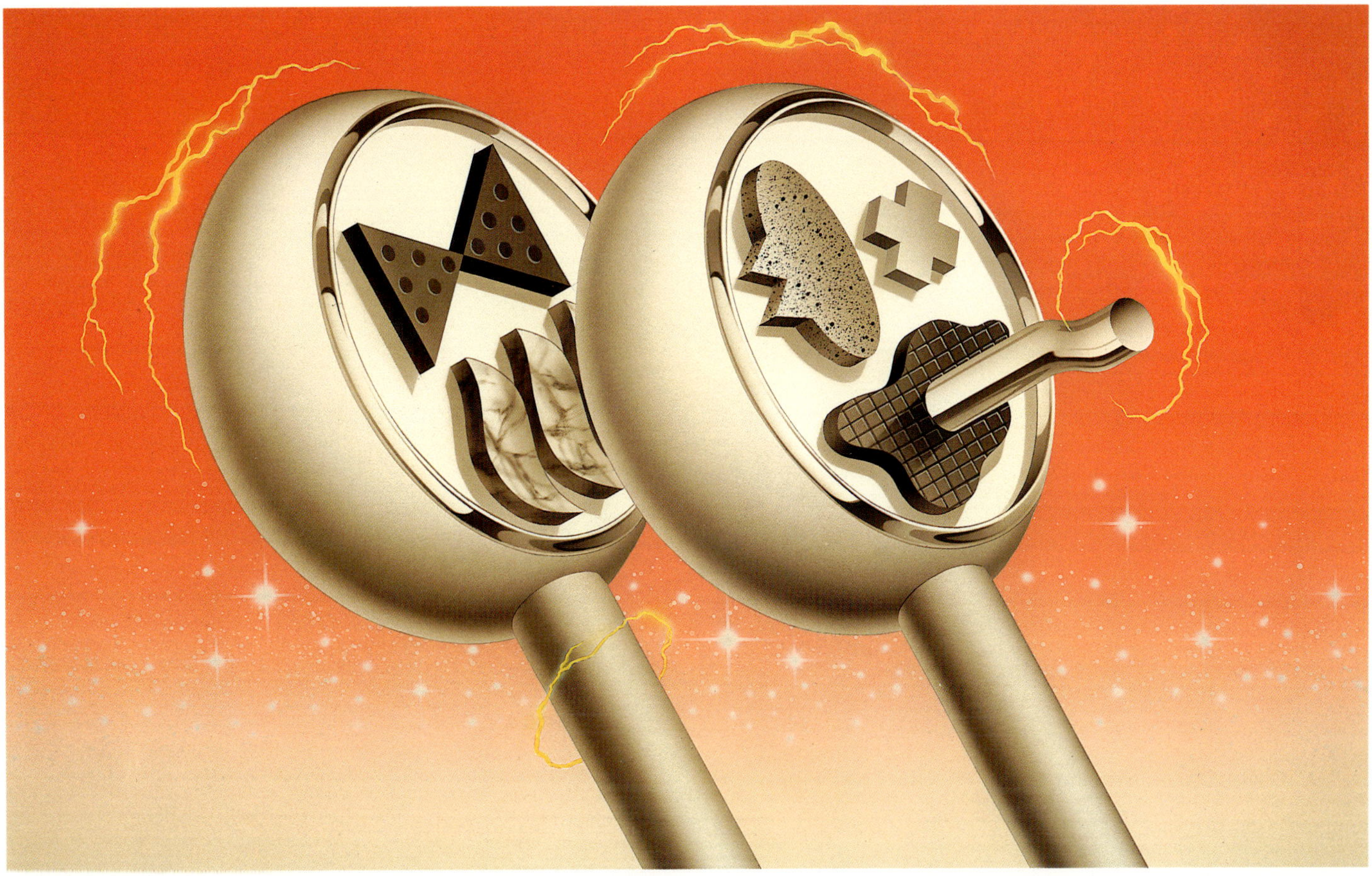

Hiroshi Aiura

Paircity Renaissance 123
24-55 Takanawa 4-chome
Minato-ku
Tokyo 108
Japan
Tel. 03-441 4958

Hiroshi Aiura

Paircity Renaissance 123
24-55 Takanawa 4-chome
Minato-ku
Tokyo 108
Japan
Tel. 03-441 4958

Illustrators Salmon

Dai 33 Fujii Building
3-7 Hiragishi
Toyohira-ku
Sapporo 062
Japan
Tel. 011-823 8971

This is a production group of professional illustrators with outside members working for them. They are available for almost any kind of illustration required by clients.

Has a wide stock of original works; illustrations, Japanese and western paintings and wood prints. They can be loaned to clients' needs. Has published and artbook, "Salmon Artists Anual 1".

Illustrators Salmon

Dai 33 Fujii Building
3-7 Hiragishi
Toyohira-ku
Sapporo 062
Japan
Tel. 011-823 8971

This is a production group of professional illustrators with outside members working for them. They are available for almost any kind of illustration required by clients.

Has a wide stock of original works; illustrations, Japanese and western paintings and wood prints. They can be loaned to clients' needs. Has published and artbook, "Salmon Artists Anual 1".

Masato Okazaki

Blue Moon Studio
D-106 Senriyama Royal Plaza
4-39 Senriyama Nishi
Suita-shi
Osaka 565
Japan
Tel. 06-339 4149
Fax: 06-339 4150

Blue Moon
Studio

Shigeyuki Sakaguchi

Clark Kent
402 Green Plaza Takatsu
15-18 Nipponbashi 2-chome
Minami-ku
Osaka 542
Japan
Tel. 06-643 1431
     644 4438
Fax: 06-644 6059

Staff:
Kosei Ichiki
Shigeki Fujimoto
Hiroko Kamiya

Technical Illustration House
CLARK KENT
(06)643-1431 644-4438

ADIA 8 1987 © Shigeyuki Sakaguchi

Ikuo Togawa

Atom
303 Kitatenma Royal Heights
5-3 Tenma 3-chome
Kita-ku
Osaka 530
Japan
Tel. 06-354 0628
Fax: 06-358 1985

Hong Kong
Hongkong
Hong Kong

ILLUSTRATORS

Fung, Karl 184
Keng Seng Trading & Co. 188
Lui, Michael 185
Ma (Shannon Ma), Fu Keung 183
Pokan Designs 187
Yuen, Tai Yung 186

Fu Keung Ma (Shannon Ma)

32A, 10/F, Un Chau Street
Sham Shui Po
Kowloon
Hong Kong
Tel. 3-87 61 51
    3-728 89 63
Pager: 3-7290222 call 2878

Agent:
Accurate Illustration Studio
32A, 4/F, Un Chau Street
Sham Shui Po
Kowloon
Hong Kong
Tel. 3-728 89 63
    87 61 51

Illustrations and retouching.

Illustrations et retouches.

Illustrationen und Retuschen.

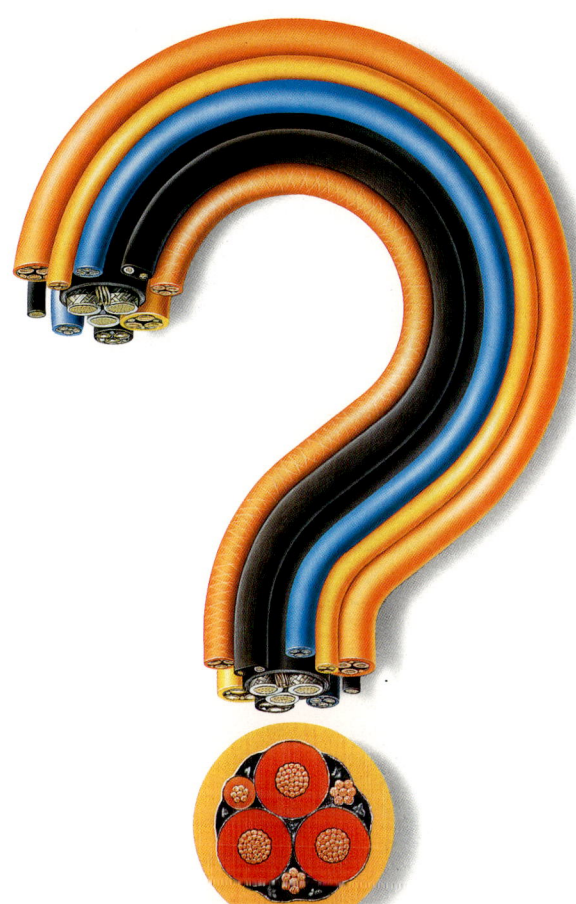

Karl Fung

Karl Studio
18-D Fu King Yuen
Chi Fu Fa Yuen
Pokfulam
Hong Kong
Tel. 5-50 10 70
Pager: 3-320251/1070

Illustrator.

Michael Lui

Michael Lui Illustration

1601, Chit Lee Commercial Building
30-36 Shaukeiwan Road
Hong Kong
Tel. 5-60 93 57

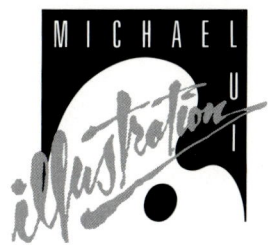

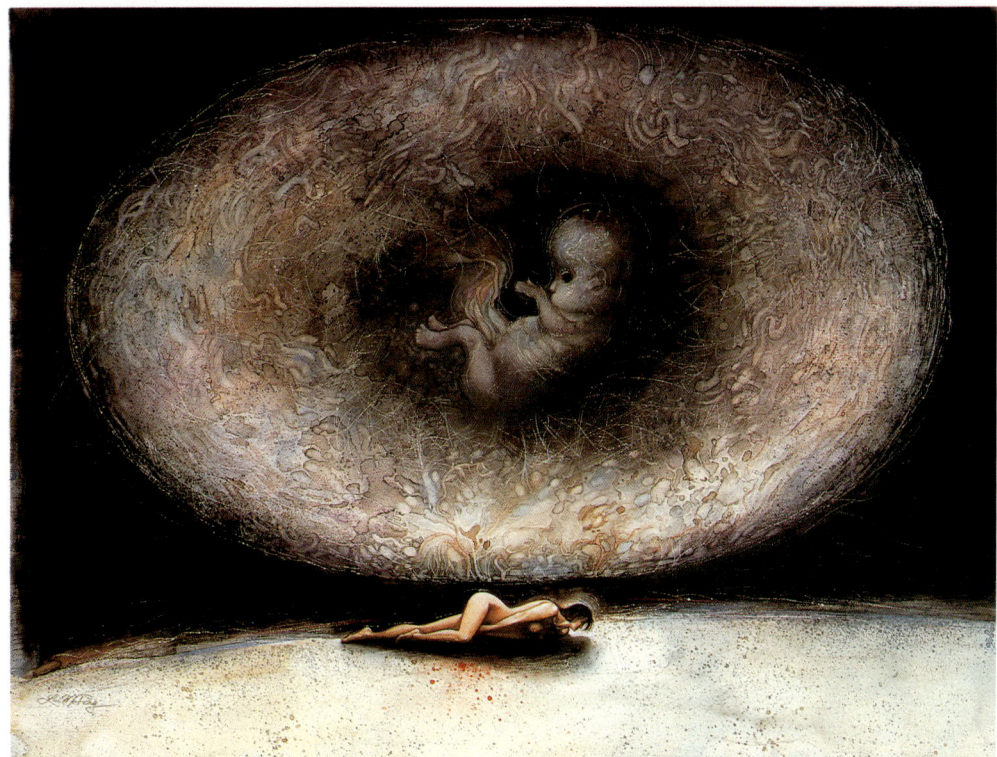

Tai Yung Yuen

Room 103
Loong San Building
140-142 Connaught Road
Central
Hong Kong
Tel. 5-45 50 08
Telex: 64820 kshk hx

Illustrator.   Illustrateur.   Illustrator.

Pokan Designs

2 Wing Fung Street, West
1/F
Wanchai
Hong Kong
Tel. 5-28 07 35

Paul B.L. Chang
Hon-Cheung Chui
Rocky C.Y. Ng

Illustration – props production – photo retouch – window display – decoration.

OCEAN PARK

STANDARD CHARTERED BANK

COMMERCIAL PRESS

PARK'N SHOP

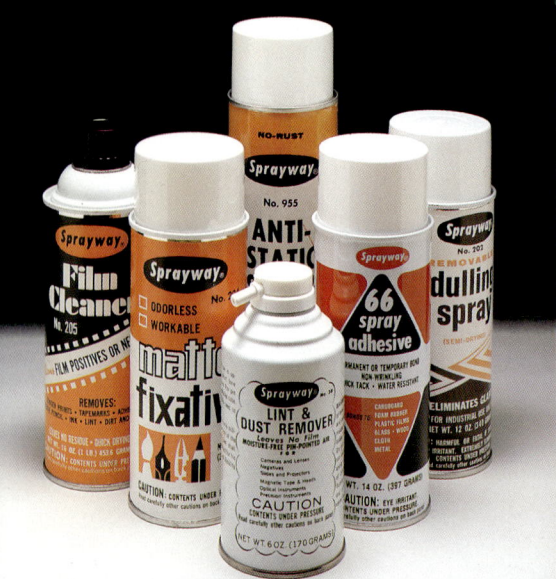

SPRAYWAY SPRAY

Matte Fixative
Anti-static Spray
Dulling Spray
Film Cleaner
66 Spray Adhesive
Lint & Dust remover

無光澤保護劑
靜電防止劑
啞面效果噴劑
菲林清潔劑
噴霧黏著劑
塵埃清除劑

ARTIFICIAL ICE

Display Ice
Photo Ice (with bubbles)
Photo Ice
Wedges Ice
Shard Ice
Crushed Ice
Soda Ice

陳列用假冰
有氣泡假冰
攝影用假冰
凹凸型假冰
碎假冰
硫打假冰

ADC mini-pro

Size: 3.9 × 16 × 12.4 cm
Weight: 280 g.
Battery: UM-2 1.5V × 4

體積：3.9×16×12.4公分
重量：280克
電源：UM-2型1.5V電池4個

BACKGROUND & GRADATION PAPER

BD Background paper
107" × 36 ft.
52" × 36 ft.
ADC Gradation paper
275 × 400 mm
400 × 550 mm
550 × 800 mm
1080 × 1560 mm
1890 × 3000 mm

背景紙
107吋×36呎
52吋×36呎
漸變色紙
275 × 400mm
400 × 550mm
550 × 800mm
1080 × 1560mm
1890 × 3000mm

ROTOVISION PUBLICATION

Photo Annual
Design Annual

設計年鑑
攝影年鑑

KENG SENG TRADING & CO.

Rm. 103, LOONG SAN BUILDING,
140-142 CONNAUGHT ROAD CENTRAL, HONG KONG.
SHEUNG WAN P.O. BOX 33723
TEL: 5-455008 5-458870
CABLE ADDRESS : KSTANDBOOK
TELEX : 64820 KSHK HX
FAX : 5-414025

競成貿易行
香港中環干諾道中140-142號隆山大廈103室
電話：5-455008 5-458870
上環郵箱 33723
電掛：KSTANDBOO
電傳：64820 KSHK H

ILLUSTRATORS

Malaysia
Malaisie
Malaysia

Flo Enterprise Sdn. Bhd. 194
Jamil, Zainuddin & Hassan, Mohd. 192
Stan Designers/Illustrators 191
Taib, Jaafar 193
Yusof, Azman 190

Azman Yusof

Creative Enterprise Sdn. Bhd.
11 A 2, Bangunan Uda
Jalan Pantai Baru
59200 Kuala Lumpur
Malaysia
Tel. 03-627 17 20
      755 43 35

Offering a wide range of styles in all forms of visual art such as airbrush art and illustration for press and advertising, children's books and comic strips.
Award:
Minor award in Capital Insurance Exhibition 1985.

Propose une grande variété de styles dans toutes les formes de l'art visuel, comme l'aérographe et l'illustration pour la presse et la publicité, les livres d'enfants et les dessins animés.
Récompense:
Prix 1985 de l'exposition «Capital Insurance».

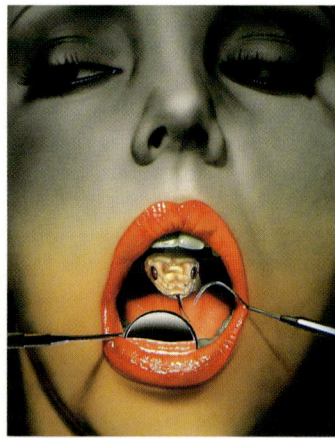

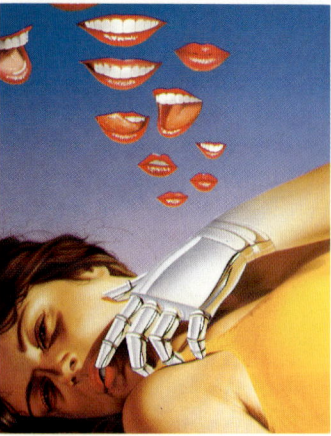

COLOUR SEPARATION BY METRO-ENGRAVERS SDN. BHD.
A73, SALAK SOUTH GARDEN, 57100 K.L., MALAYSIA.

Stan Designers/Illustrators

199, Persiaran Zaaba
Taman Tun Dr. Ismail
60000 Kuala Lumpur
Malaysia
Tel. 03-718 22 27
　　　717 29 72
Fax: 03-717 21 07

Artists representative.

1. Agency:
   Mojo. MDA Pte Ltd
   Art Director: Patricia Leong
2. Personal greeting card
3. Agency:
   The Ball Partnership Sdn Bhd
   Art Director: Kins Lee
4. Self-promotion piece.
5. Agency:
   Li Izzuldin Associates Sdn Bhd
   Client:
   Amanah Chase Merchant Bank Bhd
   Creative Director: Malkit Singh
6. Agency:
   Mojo. MDA Pte Ltd
   Art Director: Shali Rosdi

1. John Wong

2. Stan Lee

3. Sam Leong

4. Tron

5. Hou

6. Stan Lee

Zainuddin Jamil & Mohd. Hassan

Design Unit
Dewan Bahasa Dan Pustaka
50962 Kuala Lumpur
Malaysia
Tel. 03-248 10 11 Ext. 327

Zainuddin Jamil (top three pictures): Self-taught artist. Illustrations in oil, acrylic, watercolour.

Awards:
Noma Concours for children's picture book illustrations, ACCU Tokyo 1980-1986 (Runner-up).

Mohd. Hassan (bottom four pictures): Illustrations in oil, acrylic, watercolour.

Award:
Citrabudi (Runner-up) 1985.

COLOUR SEPARATION BY METRO-ENGRAVERS SDN. BHD.
A73, SALAK SOUTH GARDEN, 57100 K.L., MALAYSIA.

Jaafar Taib

Creative Enterprise Sdn. Bhd.
11 A 2, Bangunan Uda
Jalan Pantai Baru
59200 Kuala Lumpur
Malaysia
Tel. 03-657 77 67
     755 43 35

Specialized in high quality creative production. Artist, illustrator and cartoonist. His paintings appeared in Reader's Digest, Esso calendar, Toshiba calendar and were also used by various major publishing houses and agencies.
Award: Major award at Capital Insurance Exhibition 1985.

Spécialisé dans la production créative de haut niveau. Artiste, illustrateur et dessinateur de bandes dessinées. Ses peintures ont paru dans le Reader's Digest, les calendriers Esso et Toshiba et ont été utilisées par les plus grandes maisons d'édition et agences.

Récompenses:
Grand prix 1985 de l'exposition «Capital Insurance».

ILLUSTRATORS

Thailand
Thaïlande
Thailand

Punnopatham, Chotiwat 196

Chotiwat Punnopatham

310/14 Chareonrath Road
Klongsan
Bangkok 10600
Thailand
Tel. 438 30 08
    438 20 26

Illustration
Graphic Design
Packaging Design
Creative artwork

ILLUSTRATORS

New Zealand
Nouvelle-Zélande
Neuseeland

Bennett, Jeremy 203
Fuller, Stephen 201
IDA 198

Mindseye Graphics Ltd 200
Primrose, Craig Steven 199
Reed, Grant 202

NEW ZEALAND'S
TOP ILLUSTRATORS AND DESIGNERS

THE ILLUSTRATORS AND DESIGNERS ASSOCIATION PO BOX 47·371 AUCKLAND 1 NEW ZEALAND.

Craig Steven Primrose

45 Coldham Crescent
St. Johns Park
Remuera
Auckland 5
New Zealand
Tel. 09-581 332

Craig is a freelance illustrator/visualizer, specializing in all forms of illustrative work, ranging from full-colour to full-tone black and white illustrations, including concept boards, visuals and architectural perspectives.

Mindseye Graphics Ltd

10 Roxburgh Street New Market
P.O. Box 37500
Parnell
Auckland
New Zealand
Tel. 09-502 585

All illustrations by Peter Stafford.
Specializing in illustration and
graphic design.

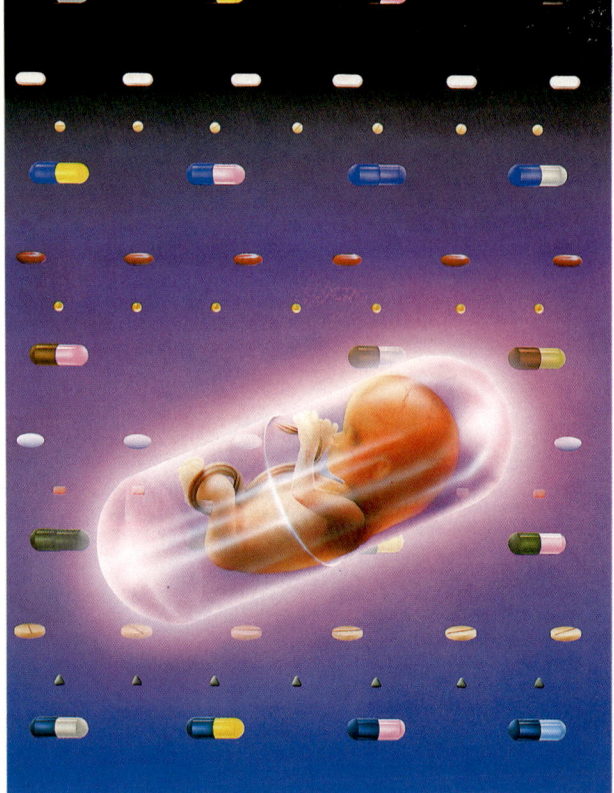

Client: ADIS PRESS

Client: ADIS PRESS

Stephen Fuller

The Advertising Picture Company Ltd
P.O. Box 973
Wellington
New Zealand
Tel. 04-873 826

Specializing in:
Illustration, design, visualizing, storyboards and packaging.

Spécialisé dans:
l'illustration, le graphisme, la visualisation, les scénarios et l'emballage.

Grant Reed

PO Box 48-141
Blockhouse Bay – Auckland
New Zealand
Tel. 09-545 000

Product, automotive and nautical illustration. Illustrative visualizing and storyboards.

Jeremy Bennett

20 Carolyne Street
Mt. Victoria
P.O. Box 9181
Wellington
New Zealand
Tel. 847 118
　　847 136

Illustration for advertising and publication. Portfolio includes specialized scraperboard and watercolour work.

Illustration pour publicité et publications. Le portfolio comprend du matériel de gravure spécialisé et des aquarelles.

Illustration für Werbung und Verlagsprodukte. Das Portfolio enthält Stiche und Aquarelle.

Australia
Australie
Australien

Golding, Michael 207
Taylor, Lynda 206

ILLUSTRATORS

Lynda Taylor

327 Darebin Road
Thornbury
Melbourne
Victoria 3071 – Australia
Tel. 03-49 1258

Agent:
The Talent Store
24/37 Albert Road
Melbourne 3004 – Australia
Tel. 03-266 2443

Michael Golding

41 Cambridge Street
Paddington
Sydney, NSW 2021 – Australia
Tel. 02-333 949

207

ILLUSTRATORS

Turkey / Turquie / Türkei

Ateş, Metin 211
Berktav, Sedat 211
Bilir, Fuat 211
Çatak, Necdet 211
Deniz, İlkin 211
Erman, Ahmet 211
Özcan, İskender 211

The winning illustrations are for the "ART DIRECTORS" INDEX TO ILLUSTRATION, GRAPHICS & DESING No. 8" Competition.

This competition was organized by the BILIMSEL ESERLER, TURKEY

Taksim, Sıraselviler Caddesi, Ayla İş Hanı
No. 66 Daire 4, İSTANBUL/TURKEY
Phones: (1) 143 41 73, 149 96 33, 149 47 87
Telex: 25963 bies tr Fax: 149 47 87

Metin Ateş	Bekârbey Sok. No. 16/1 Davutpaşa, Aksaray/İstanbul Tel: (1) 523 89 41
Sedat Berktav	Kuyumcu İrfan Sok. No: 26/2 Nişantaşı/İstanbul Tel: (1) 130 69 80-(1) 140 78 34
Fuat Bilir	Alaca Mescid Cad. hamam Sok. Çıkmazı, Yeni Okcular İşhanı, Kat: 1 No: 7 Okcular/Bursa Tel: (241) 15009
Necdet Çatak	Altıyol, Çilek Sok, Akyol İşhanı, No: 16/1 Kadıköy/İstanbul Tel: (1) 345 45 00
İlkin Deniz	Kayışdağı Cad. Aykın Ap. No: 141/1 Daire: 10 Kadıköy/İstanbul Tel: (1) 346 03 53
Ahmet Erman	Etemefendi Cad. Değerbilir Sok. No: 18, Daire: 7 Erenköy/İstanbul Tel: (1) 360 74 26
İskender Özcan	Hızırbey Cad. 2. Bülbül Sok. No: 9/4 Hasanpaşa/İstanbul Tel: (1) 149 96 33

Sedat Berktav

İlkin Deniz

Necdet Çatak

İskender Özcan

Ahmet Erman

İskender Özcan

Metin Ateş

Fuat Bilir

Belgium
Belgique
Belgien

Maris, Luc 215
Trias Creative Team bvba 214

ILLUSTRATORS

Trias Creative Team bvba

Tulpstraat 4
B–2008 Antwerpen
Tel. 03-231 75 60

Conctact:
Georges Van Tilburgh

B&W and colour retouching
Hyper realistic artworks
Airbrush artworks
Illustrations

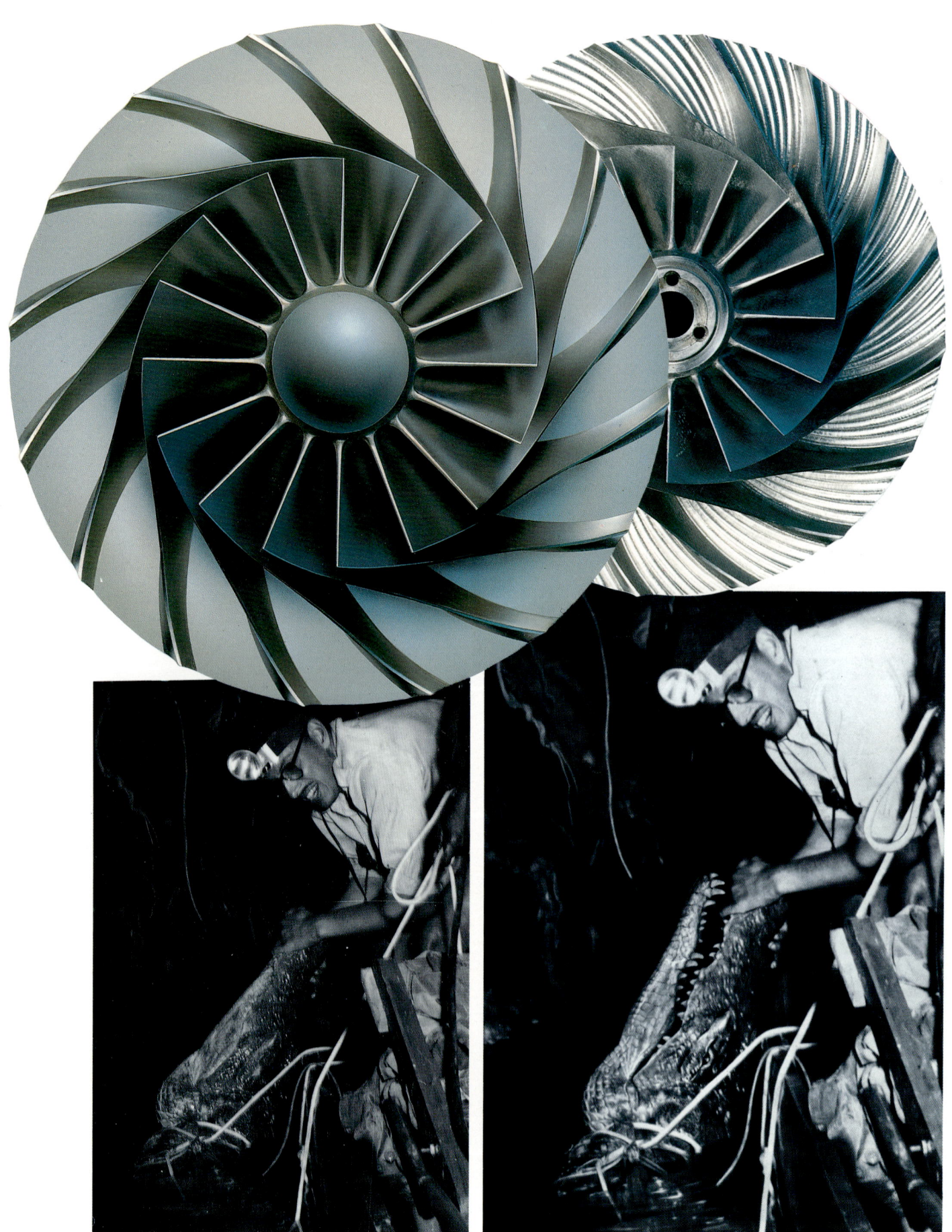

Luc Maris

Theodoor Van Rijswijck Plaats 7
B–2000 Antwerpen
Tel. 03-232 41 55

Agent:
Drukkerij & Uitgeverij Roels N.V.
Hogeweg 10-16
B–2200 Borgerhout
Tel. 03-235 90 96
Telex 33882 r.print B
Telefax 03.235.37.62

Free-lance illustrator and graphic designer.
Specialized in covers, calendars, portrait, nature illustrations, posters and typographic layouts.

Free-lance illustrator en grafisch ontwerper.
Gespecialiseerd in covers, kalenders, portret, natuurillustraties, affiches en typografische lay-out.

Illustrateur et graphiste indépendant.
Spécialisé dans les couvertures, calendriers, portraits, illustrations de nature, affiches et montages typographiques.

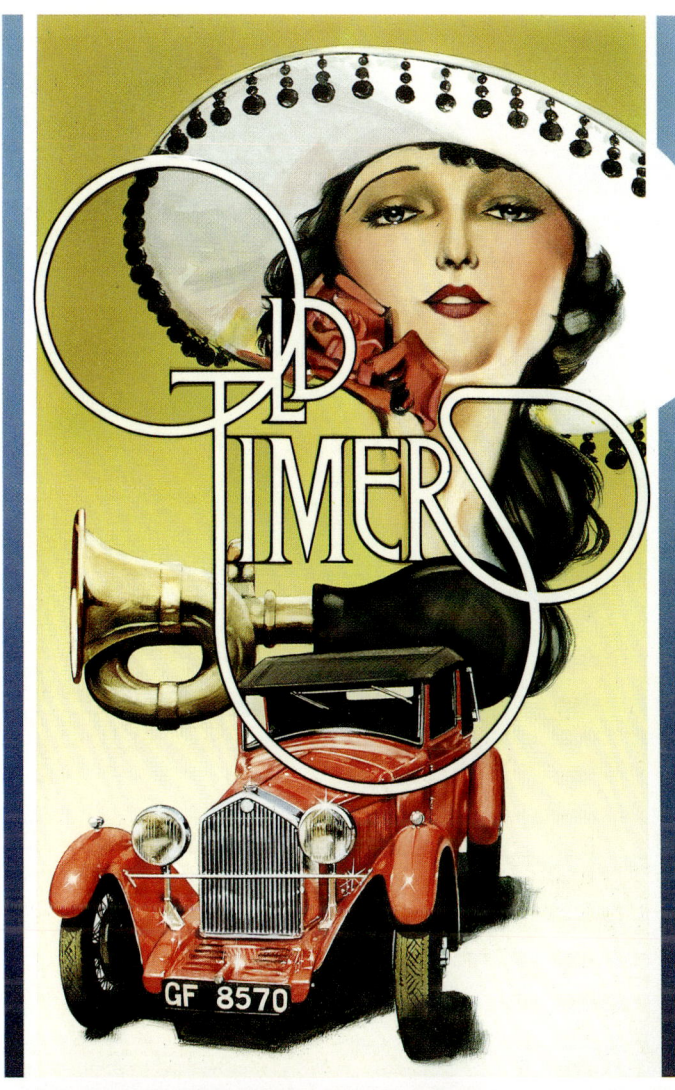

Holland
Hollande
Holland

ILLUSTRATORS

Boogaard, Ronald van den 222
Idetif Graphic 218-219
Van Den Oord, Hans 220
Virgo Design 221

Idetif Graphic

All-round Illustratieburo
Idetif-Graphic bv
Vossendaal 51
Postbus 272
NL–4870 AG Etten-Leur
Tel. 01659-3457
     4697
Fax: 01659-3243

All-round en professioneel illustratieburo, team van 8 vaste en 4 freelance medewerkers, veelzijdig maar toch gespecialiseerd.
Vraag om een vrijblijvende presentatie van het werk.

All-round professional illustration bureau.
A team of 8 full-time personnel and 4 freelance, versatile and individually specialized.
Ask for free work samples.

Bureau d'illustrateurs professionnels dans tous les domaines. Equipe de 8 collaborateurs fixes et de 4 indépendants, polyvalents quoique spécialisés.
Demandez des exemples gratuits de notre travail.

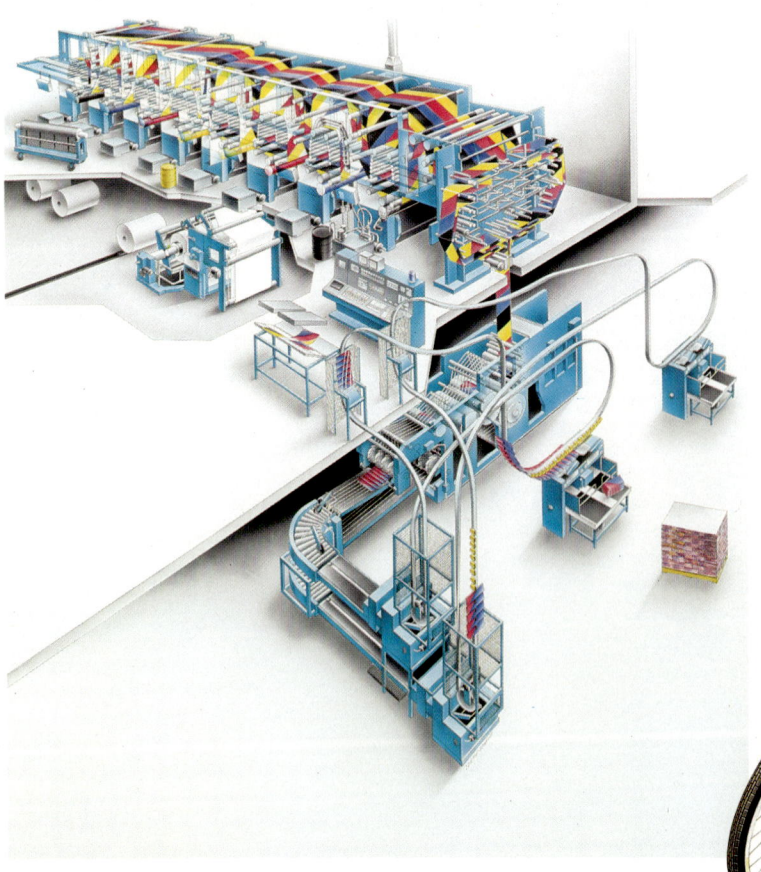

Idetif Graphic

All-round Illustratieburo
Idetif-Graphic bv
Vossendaal 51
Postbus 272
NL–4870 AG Etten-Leur
Tel. 01659-3457
       4697
Fax: 01659-3243

All-round Illustrations-Atelier.
Team von 8 fest angestellten und
4 unabhängigen Mitarbeitern,
vielseitig und doch spezialisiert.
Fordern Sie unkostenfreie
Arbeitsbeispiele an.

Oficina de ilustradores
profesionales en todas esferas.
Equipo de 8 colaboradores fijos y
de 4 independientes, polivalentes
aunque especialistas.
Pida Vd. ejemplos gratuitos de
nostro trabajo.

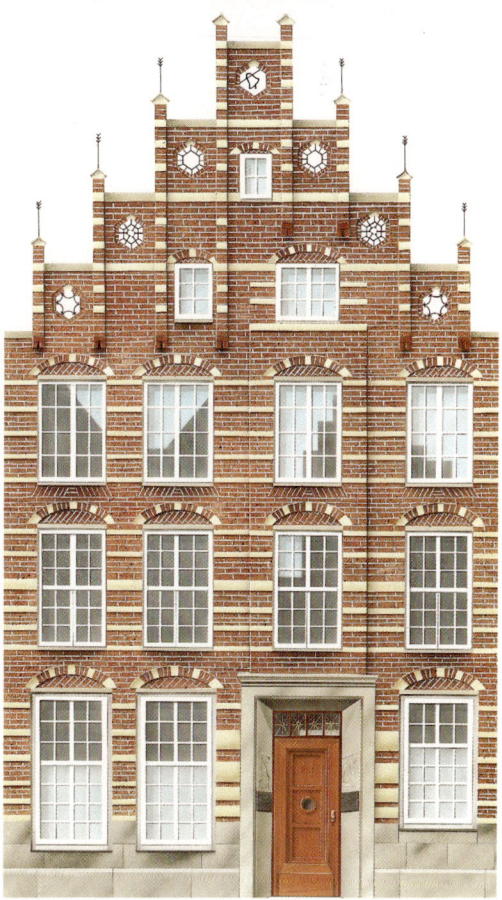

Hans Van Den Oord

Tel. 070-50 39 12
     070-45 62 69

Agent:
Cart'ell Graphic Creations
Seinpoststraat 70
NL–2586 HC Den Haag
Tel. 070-50 58 77
Fax: 070-50 48 99

Illustrations	Illustraties	Illustrationen
Photo retouch	Fotoretouch	Fotoretusche
Graphic design	Graphic design	Grafisches Design

Virgo Design

Vondelstraat 154
NL–1054 GT Amsterdam
Tel. 020-18 74 20
Fax: 020-18 26 56

Graphic creation, illustrations, visuals, ready artwork and printing follow-up.

Grafische vormgeving, illustraties, visuals, werktekeningen en drukwerkbegeleiding.

Grafische Gestaltung, Illustration, Anschauungsmittel, Reinzeichnungen und Druckauftragsbetreuung.

Ronald van den Boogaard   NIC

Korte Leidsedwarsstraat 37 - 4
NL–1017 PW Amsterdam
Tel. 020-26 15 19

Clockwise: anamorfosis, display consumer loans, NMB Bank; Cover consumer brochure Pewag Snow-chains; Dealerpromotion ad, Bolfo anti-flee spray, Bayer; Poster, staff motivation campaign, NMB Bank; All these through agencies.

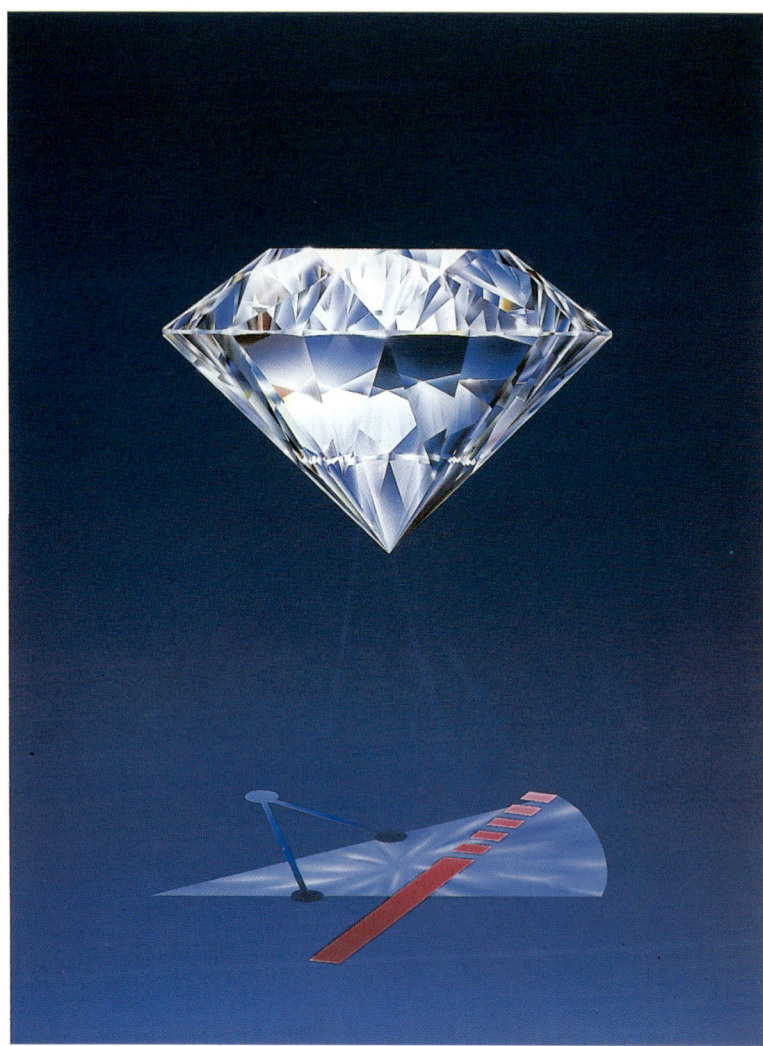

ILLUSTRATORS

Luxembourg
Luxembourg
Luxemburg

Kreutz, Will 224
Sam's & Cie 224

Sam's & Cie / Will Kreutz

Agence de publicité

Rue Heine 4
L–1720 Luxembourg
Tél. 352-49 42 42
     49 43 82

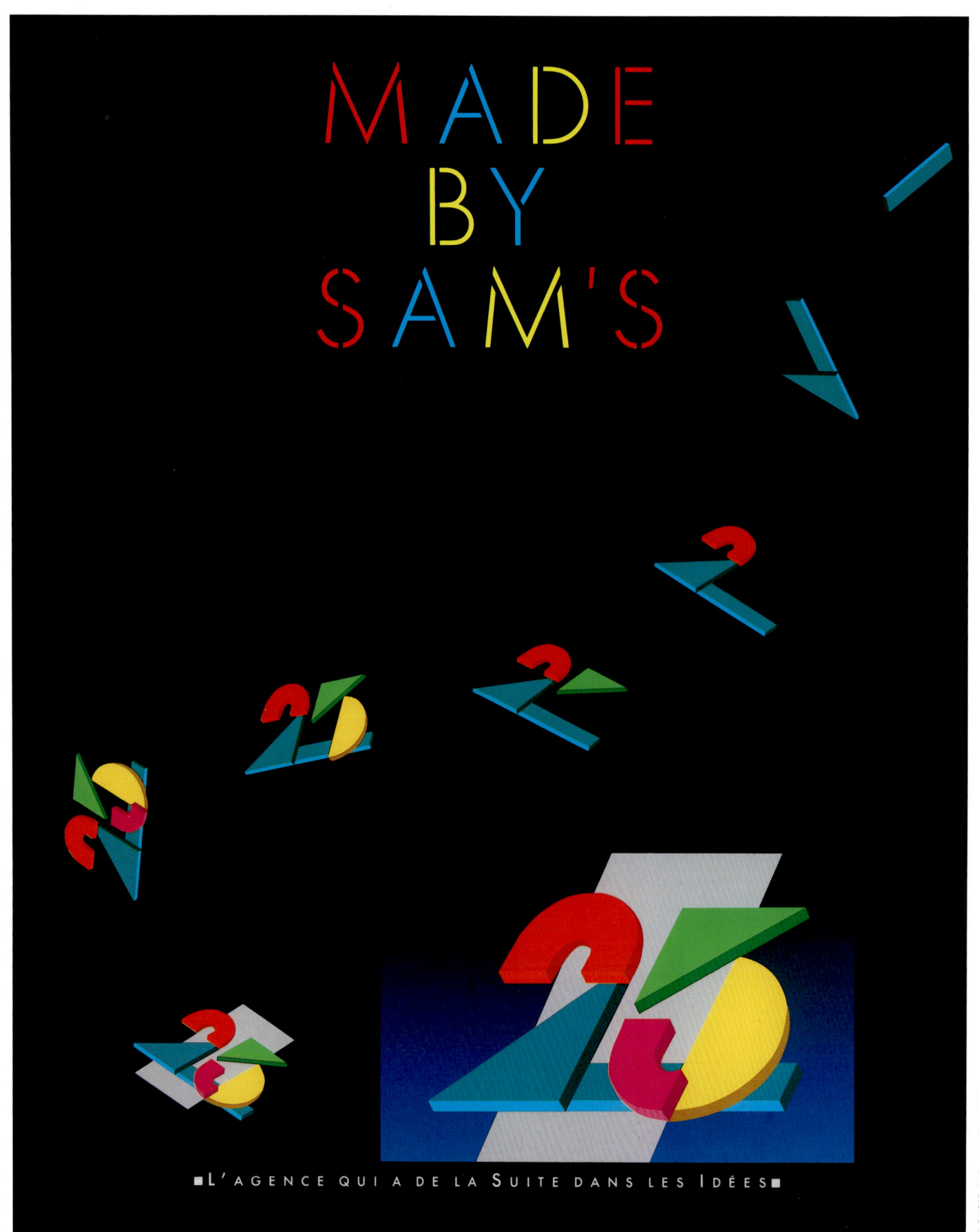

ILLUSTRATORS

France
France
Frankreich

Baffou, Patrice 227
Collier, Philipp 229
Giroud, Annie-France 228
Jacki (Jacques Tosetto) 231
Pattou, Jean 230

Patrice Baffou

9, rue de la Californie
F–37000 Tours
Tél. 47 05 40 05

Annie-France Giroud

25/27, boulevard Exelmans
F–75016 Paris
Tél. 1-45 24 61 85

Philipp Collier

Agent pour la France:
Véronique Dayle
30, avenue du Général Leclerc
F–92100 Boulogne
Tél. 1-46 05 39 27

PHILIP COLLIER: 28 AVENUE DES LILAS 59800 LILLE FRANCE TEL 20 06 39 28 TELECOPIEUR 20 47 32 50

Jean Pattou

34, place du Concert
F–59800 Lille
Tél. 20 55 77 54

Jacki (Jacques Tosetto)

132, rue du Faubourg-Poissonnière Illustrator
F–75010 Paris
Tél. 1-48 74 46 95 Sculptor
et
Le Château Conceptor
Rue du Trê
F–70130 Evry-le-Châtel
Tél. 25 70 54 76

ILLUSTRATORS

Germany
Allemagne
Deutschland

ACM 234
ApunktMpunkt 248
Biswanger, Claus D. 243
Fröschl, Andreas 245
GraphiCom GmbH 242
Hilbel, Volker 246
Lichthardt, Ulrich 240-241

Moos-Drevenstedt, Erika 244
Schüssler, Alfred 236-237
Stedtler, Lothar 238
Studio Becker GmbH 239
Towndrow, Arthur H. 235
Wohlgemuth, Stephan 247

ACM
TECHNISCHE GRAFIK & DOKUMENTATION

Lohmarer Str. 28
5210 Troisdorf
West Germany
Tel. (02241) 75113

Unten aufgeführt sind einige Beispiele unserer farblich angelegten Zeichnungen mit verschiedenen Stilarten.

Below are a few samples of our colour work and the possible styles that can be adopted.

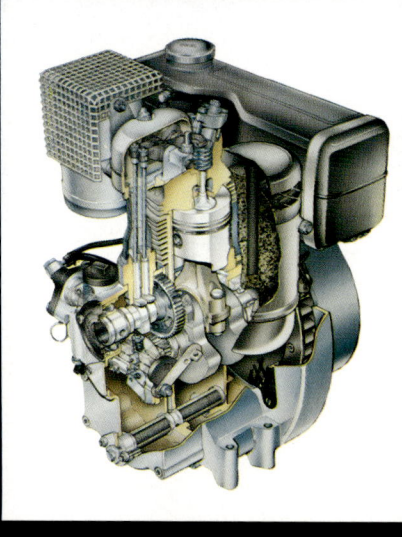
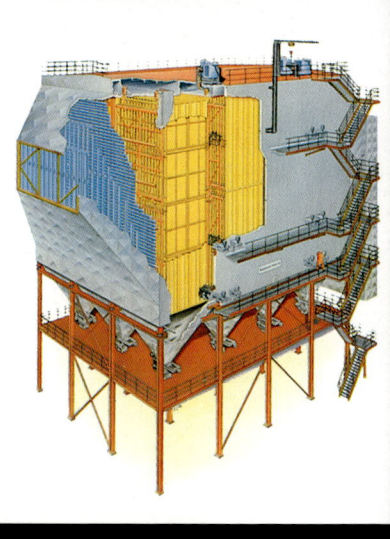
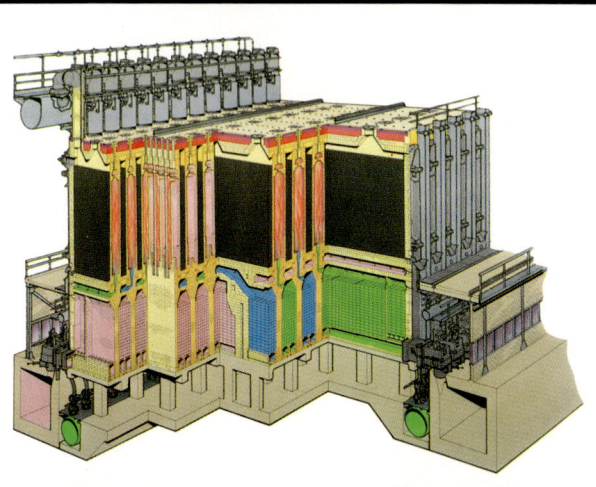

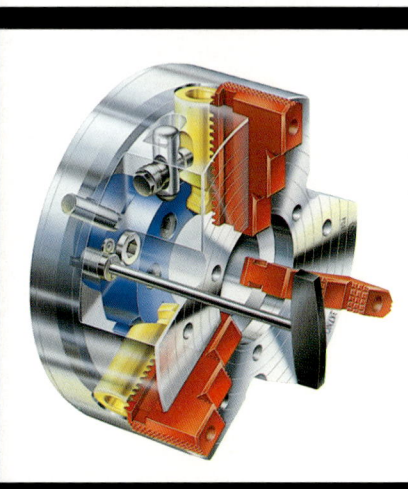

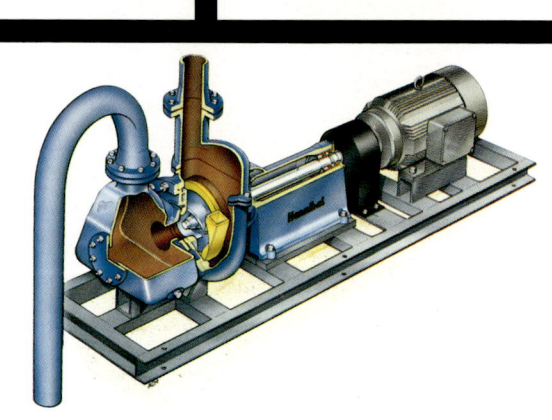

Arthur H. Towndrow

Grafisches Atelier
Bahnweg 35
D-4970 Bad Oeynhausen
Tel. 0 57 31 – 2 90 44

Alfred Schüssler

Heidestrasse 146 A
D–6000 Frankfurt am Main 60
Tel. 069-46 76 88

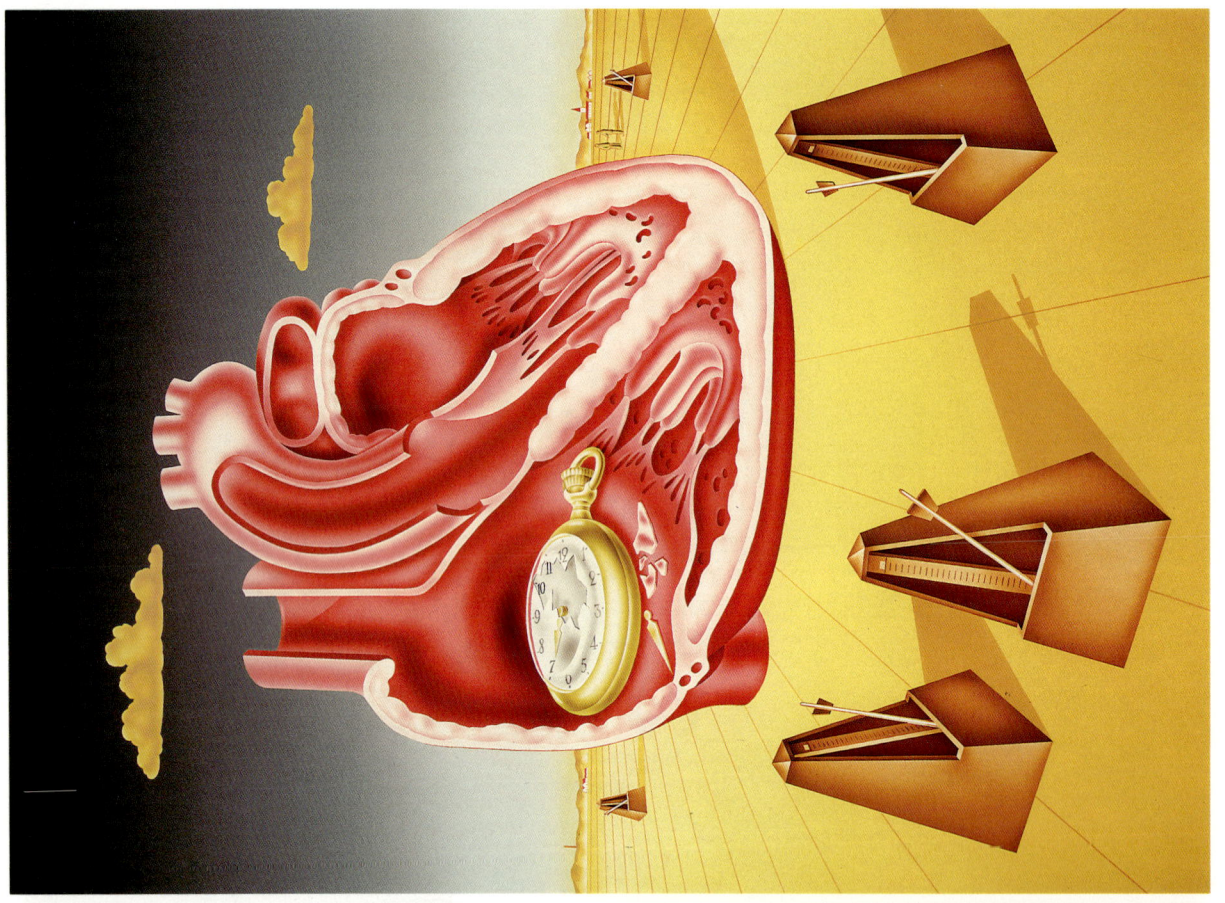

Alfred Schüssler

Heidestrasse 146 A
D-6000 Frankfurt am Main 60
Tel. 069-46 76 88

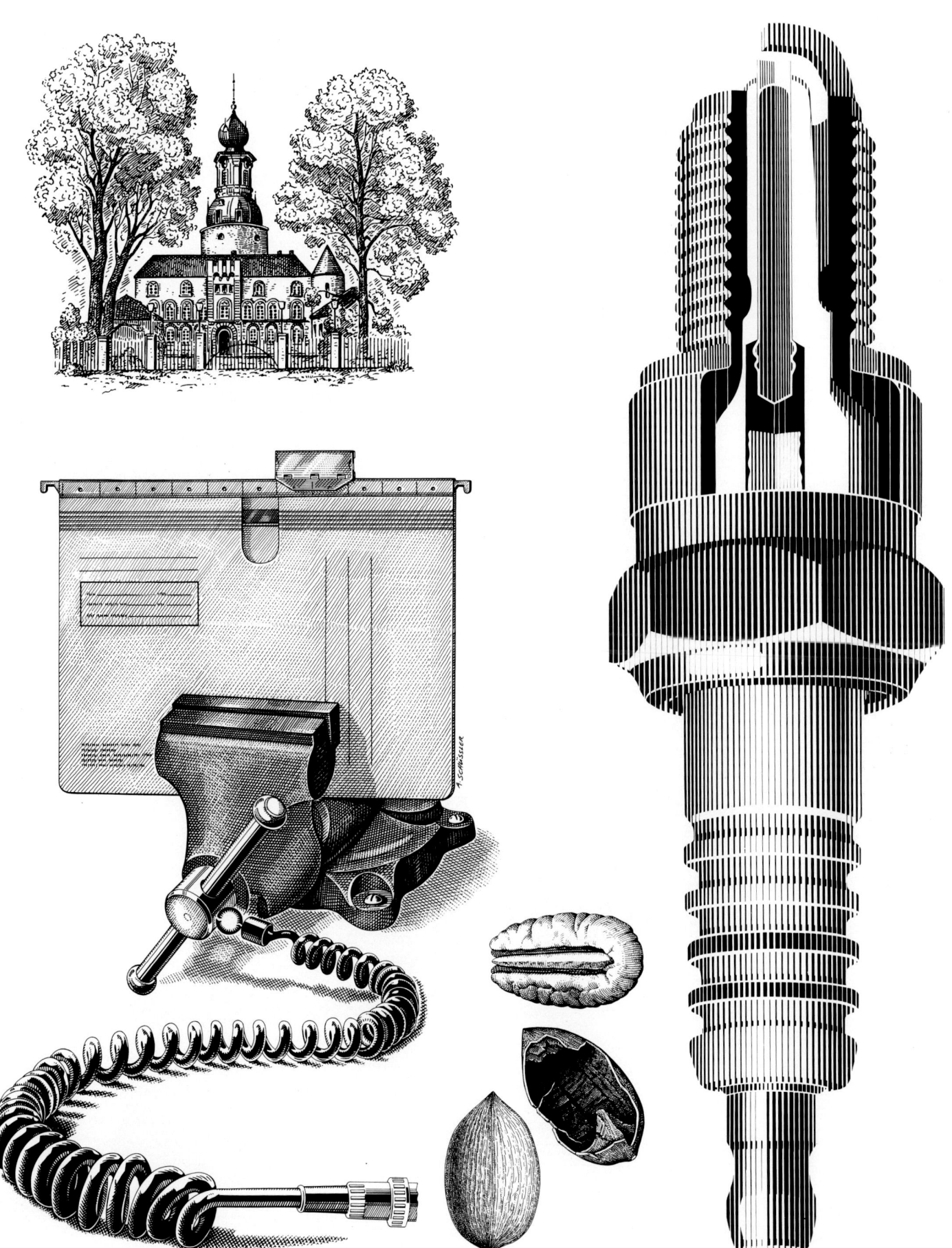

Lothar Stedtler

Art Director + Illustrator AGD

Hubertushang 5
D–5063 Overath
Tel. 02206-2664

Conception. Graphic design. Realistic illustration in the field of medicine, science and technics with airbrush or any other style you wish.

Conception. Graphisme. Illustrations réalistes dans les domaines de la médecine, des sciences et technique en aérographe ou tout autre style désiré.

Konzeption. Grafik-Design. Realistische Illustrationen im medizinischen, wissenschaftlichen und technischen Bereich in Airbrush-Technik und jeder anderen gewünschten Stilrichtung.

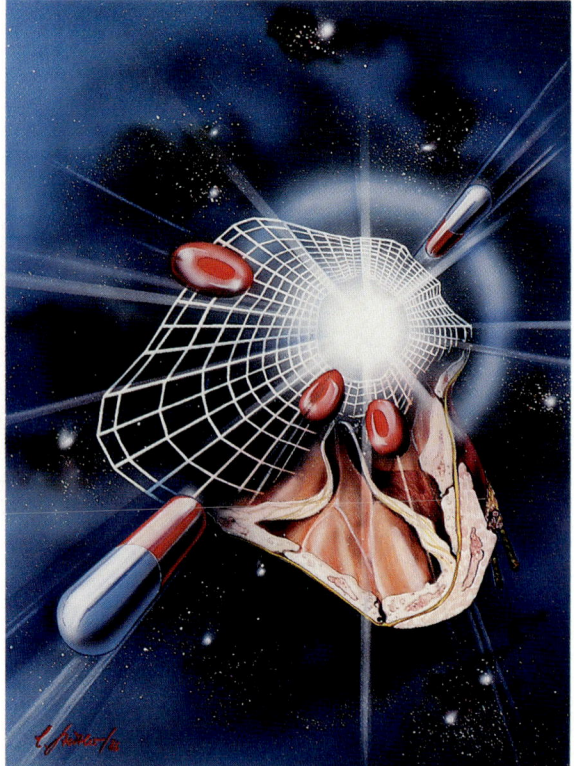

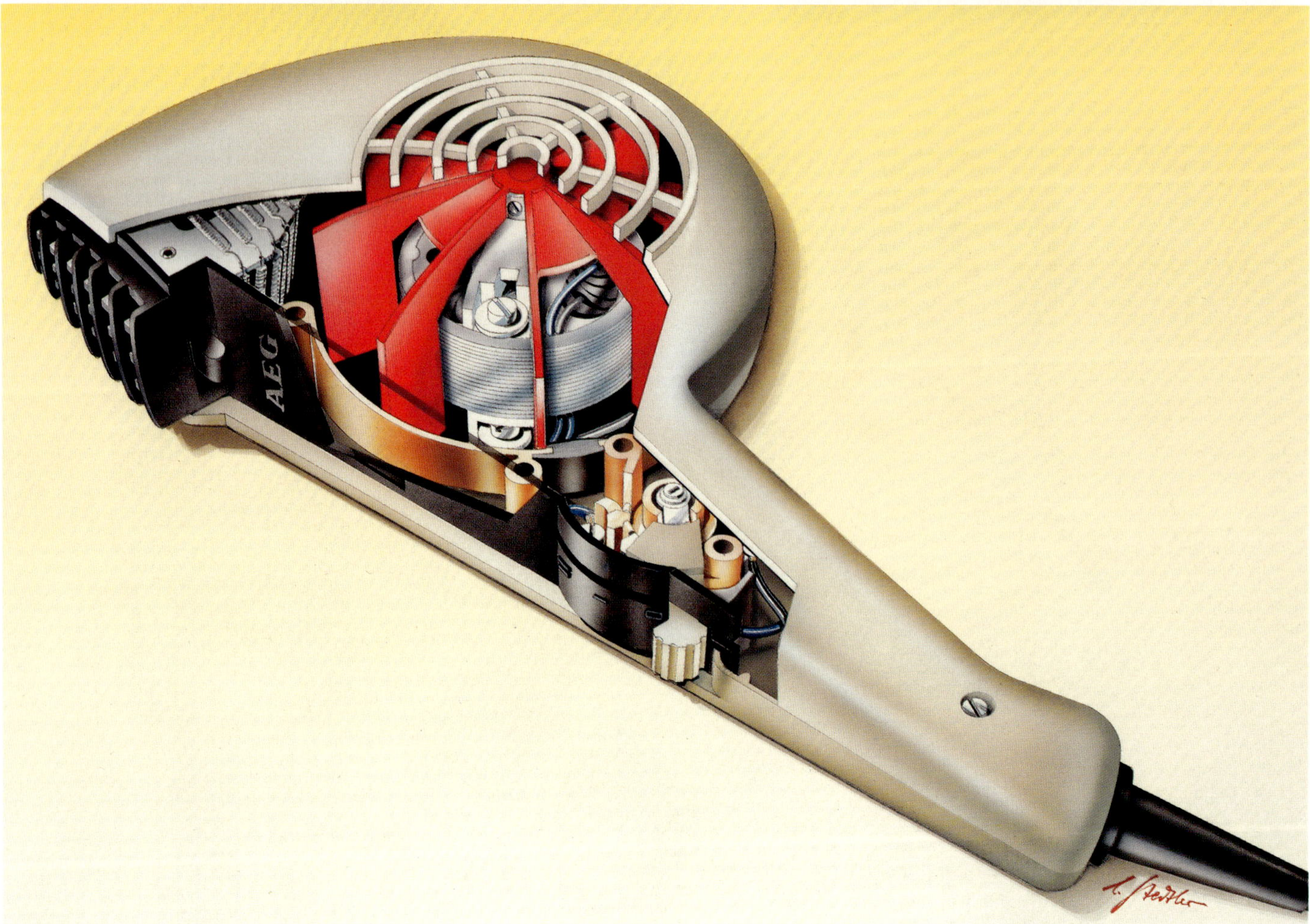

Studio Becker GmbH

Wiesenau 46
D–6000 Frankfurt/Main 1
Tel. 069-72 16 25
Telex: 4170777 beck d
Fax: 069-72 16 25
Btx: 069-72 17 08

3-D Illustrationen
Grafik Design
Kunststudium
Darmstadt

3-D illustration
Graphic Design
Art studies in
Darmstadt

3-D illustration
Design graphique
Etudes artistiques
à Darmstadt

Ulrich Lichthardt

Hohenzollernstrasse 128
D–8000 München 40
Tel. 089-30 17 72

Agent:
Lothar Poppensieker
Grillparzerstrasse 44
D–8000 München 80
Tel. 089-47 95 69

Illustrations and fashion design.

Illustrations et dessins de mode.

Illustrationen und Modezeichnungen.

Ulrich Lichthardt

Hohenzollernstrasse 128
D–8000 München 40
Tel. 089-30 17 72

Agent:
Lothar Poppensieker
Grillparzerstrasse 44
D–8000 München 80
Tel. 089-47 95 69

Illustrations and fashion design.

Illustrations et dessins de mode.

Illustrationen und Modezeichnungen.

GraphiCom GmbH

Hofkamp 87
D–5600 Wuppertal 1
Tel. 0202-493 63 01
Fax: 0202-493 63 03

Hochauflösende Computergraphik für höchste Ansprüche und viele Medien...
- Präsentation, Audiovision, Werbung, Schulung, Verkaufsförderung, Druck...
- Businessgraphik, Sachillustration, Artwork, Animation...
- Ausgabe als Dia, OH-Folie, Print...

High Resolution Computergraphics in High Level Quality for multimedia...
- Presentation, audiovisual, advertising, training, marketing support, printing...
- Businesscharts, overall illustrations, animation...
- Output: slides, transparencies, prints...

Graphisme par ordinateur à haute résolution de la meilleure qualité pour nombreux supports publicitaires...
- Présentation, audiovision, publicité, formation, promotion, impression...
- Graphisme commercial, illustration générale, originaux, animation...
- Sous forme de diapositives, feuilles transparentes, tirage papier...

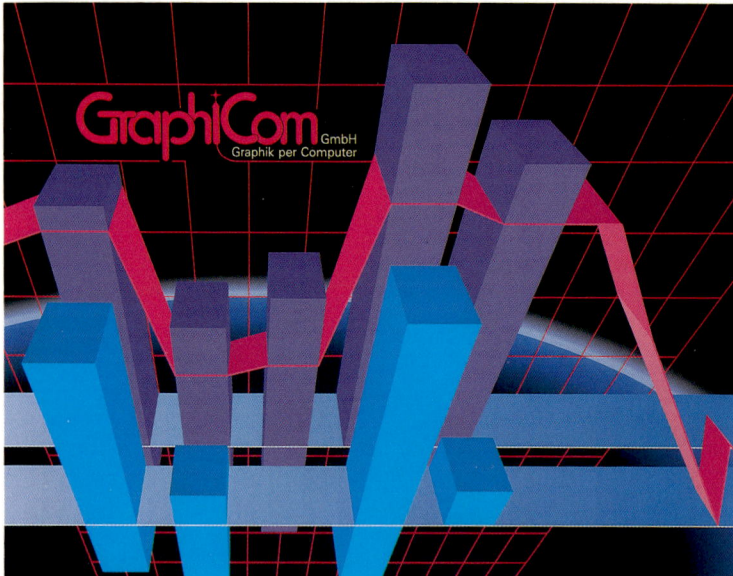
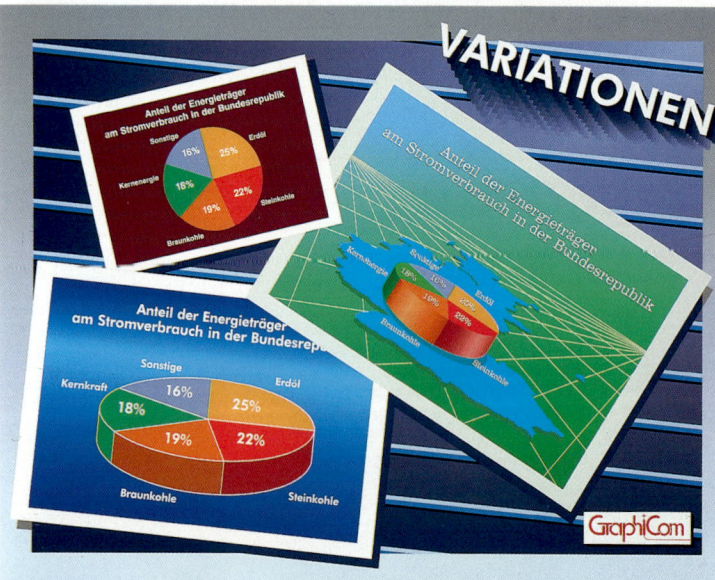

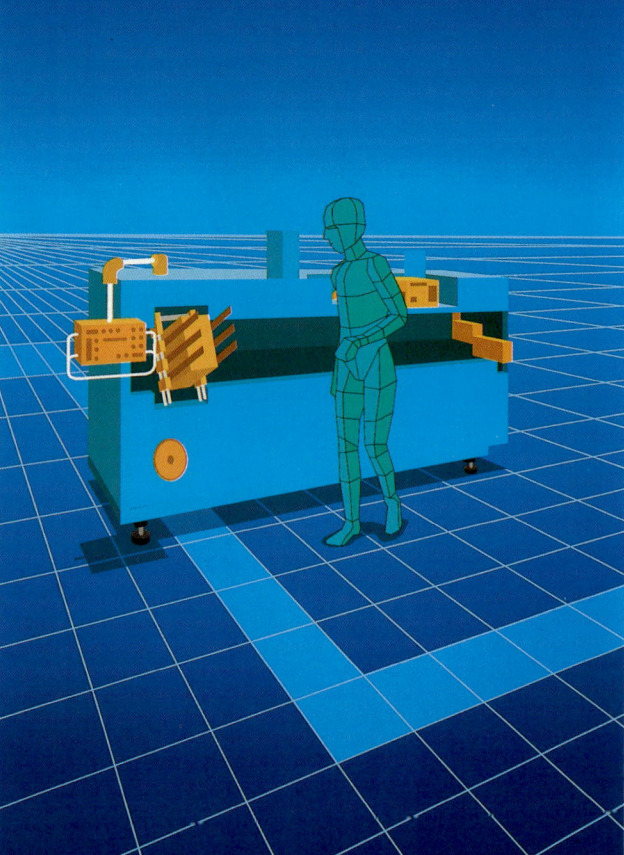
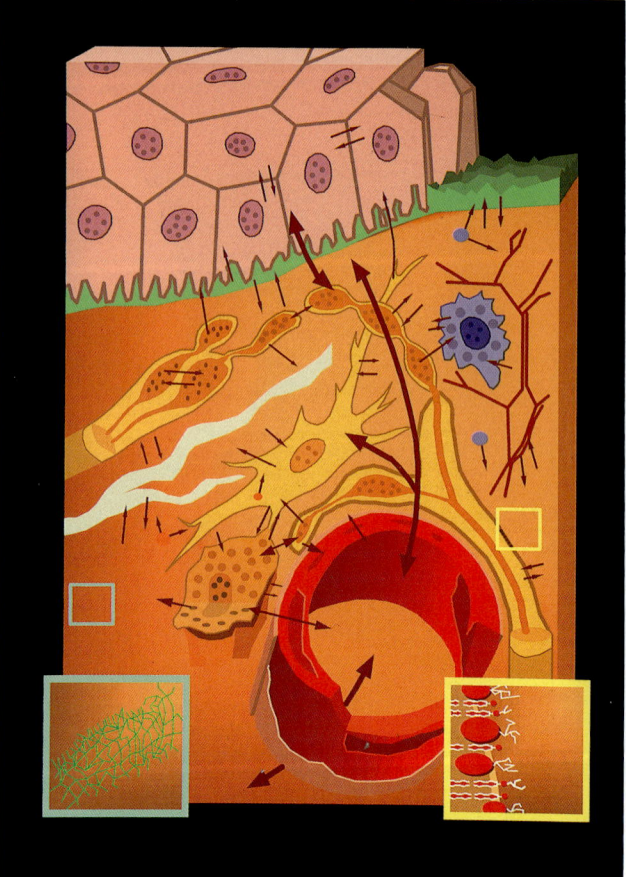

Claus D. Biswanger

Fürstenstrasse 9
D–8000 München 2
Tel. 089-28 21 93

Erika Moos-Drevenstedt

Paul-Gerhardt-Strasse 23
D-4156 Willich 2 – Anrath
Tel. 02156-38 06

Illustrations:
figurative, plants, caricature,
layout, storyboard.

Illustrations:
figuratives, plantes, caricatures,
maquettes, storyboard.

Illustration:
Figürliches, Pflanzen, Karikatur,
Layout, Storyboard.

Andreas Fröschl

L8, 13 Postfach 775
D–6800 Mannheim 1
Tel. 0621-29 13 56

Airbrush technique,
fashion drawings,
science fiction illustration.

Technique de l'aérographe,
dessins de mode,
illustration de science-fiction.

Airbrush-Technik,
Modezeichnungen,
Science Fiction Illustrationen.

Volker Hilbel

Hirmerweg 26
D–8000 München 60
Tel. 089-87 36 50

Dipl. Designer,
Art Director.
Illustrator aus Leidenschaft.
3 D-Grafik, Computergrafik.

Stephan Wohlgemuth

Steinlestrasse 32
D-6000 Frankfurt 70
Tel. 069-631 38 72

Hauptsache realistisch!

ApunktMpunkt

Horstweg 29
D–1000 Berlin 19
Tel. 030-321 40 45

Grafik & Illustration.

Denmark
Danemark
Dänemark

ILLUSTRATORS

Aardestrup, Henning 251
Beierholm, Lars 250
Blond, Jes 252
Brandt, Kjeld 253
Christensen, Ole "Flyv" 254
De Korte, Viki 255
Forup, Lennart 256
Frøjlund, Dan 257
Hedegaard, Jørgen 258
Hummeluhr, Jesper 259

3-D Illustrations 266
Kirsten + Karsten Koch 260
LM-Illustration 262-263
Madsen, Carsten 261
Oberoi, T. 267
Petagno, Joe 265
Preston, Fred 264
Spinat 250
Viby, Robert 268

Henning Aardestrup

Asåvej 21
DK-9220 Aalborg Ø
Tel. 08-15 79 10

Art direction and illustration for magazines, books and advertising.

Directeur artistique et illustrateur pour magazines, livres et publicité.

Künstlerische Leitung und Illustration von Zeitschriften, Büchern und Werbemitteln.

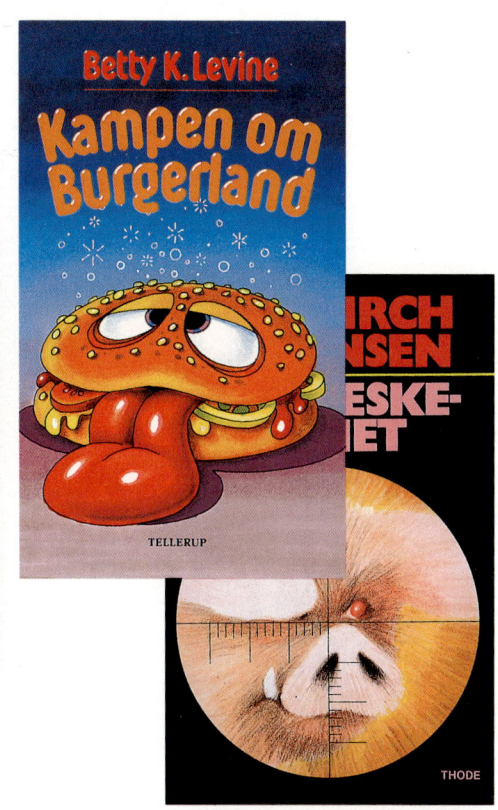

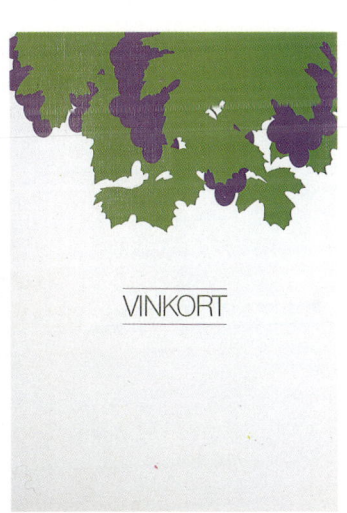

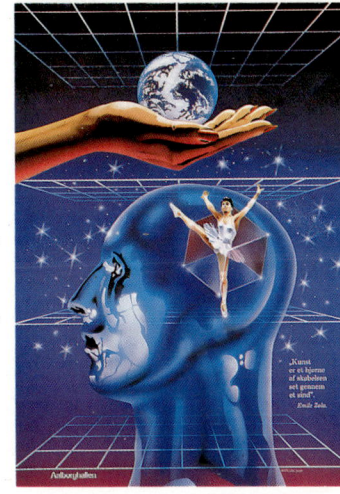

Jes Blond

St. St. Blichersgade 23
DK-8000 Århus C
Tel. 06-19 54 95

Agent:
Motivmaskinen
Hjelmensgade 31B
DK-8000 Århus C
Tel. 06-18 89 99

If ya' gotta' change — ya' gotta' change!

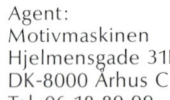

Kjeld Brandt

Kronprinsensgade 14
DK–1114 Copenhagen K
Tel. 01-13 22 60
Fax: 01-93 22 70

Born in Bornholm 1941.
The Graphic High School 1963.
The United Printers 1965.
Contact Advertising Agency 1967.
Gyldendal Publishers 1971.
Freelance since 1975.
Graphic design and illustration of any kind. I would be obliged to send further samples of my work.

Født paa Bornholm 1941.
Den Grafiske Højskole 1963.
De Forenede Trykkerier 1965.
Contact Reklamebureau 1967.
Gyldendal 1971.
Freelance 1975.
Grafisk design og illustration af enhver art. Jeg sender gerne yderligere arbejdsprøver.

Geboren 1941 auf Bornholm.
Grafische Hochschule 1963.
Vereinigte Druckereien 1965.
Contact Werbeagentur 1967.
Gyldendal-Verlag 1971.
Freischaffend seit 1975.
Grafisches Design und Illustration jeglicher Art. Gerne sende ich Ihnen weitere Arbeitsbeispiele.

Ole "Flyv" Christensen

Klokkestøbergade 8
DK-9000 Aalborg
Tel. +45-8-16 80 20

Illustration, design and art direction.

Illustration, graphisme et direction artistique.

Illustration, Grafik und Kunstdirektion.

Viki De Korte

Mejerivænget 15
DK–8310 Tranbjerg
Tel. 06-29 19 30

Own drawing office.
Mad about markers and brushes together with everything else good in this life.
My mood is at its highest when I draw:
People, fashion, advertising, food, animals, flowers, packaging, pattern design, etc.

Egen tegnestue.
Vild med tuscher og pensler, samt alt andet godt her i livet...
Humøret topper, når jeg tegner:
Mennesker, mode, reklame, mad, dyr, blomster, emballage, mønstre, m.m.

Eigenes Zeichenstudio.
Verrückt nach Farbe und Pinsel und was das Leben sonst noch Gutes bietet.
Am wohlsten ist fühle ich mich beim Zeichnen von:
Leuten, Mode, Werbung, Nahrungsmitteln, Tieren, Blumen, Verpackungen, Mustern, usw.

Lennart Forup

Ambra Allé 37
DK-2770 Kastrup
Tel. 01-50 65 51

1. Tuba Records
2. Bayer Danmark A/S
3. Magazine
4. Young & Rubicam
   (Diners Club)
   Art Director: Sonja Rasmussen
5. Book cover
   Computergrafik / Video
6. Book illustration
7, 8. Henriksen & Sieling / BBDO
   (Dansk Naturgas)
   Art Director: Claus Jørgensen

Dan Frøjlund

Horsebakken 60
DK–2400 Copenhagen NV
Tel. 01-60 06 96

Professional artwork.

Jørgen Hedegaard

Willemoesgade 9 st.
DK-2100 Copenhagen Ø
Tel. 01-42 42 90

Freelance artist specialized in graphic design and illustration for books and advertising.

Artiste indépendant spécialisé dans le design graphique, l'illustration de livres et la publicité.

Selbständiger Künstler spezialisiert auf Graphic Design und Illustration für Bücher und Werbung

Illustrationsforslag til Landsforeningen for Bedre Hørelse

Jørgen Hedegaard
Grafisk formgivning
og illustration
Tlf.: 01 42 42 90

Jesper Hummeluhr

Rosenørns Allé 33, st. tv.
DK–1970 Frederiksberg C
Tel. 01-39 02 63

I work as freelance illustrator for advertising and publishing houses, industries and magazines. Airbrush, drawings, layouts, finished artwork, posters, books, silk-screen process.

Ich arbeite als freischaffender Illustrator für Werbeagenturen und Verlagshäuser, Industrie und Zeitschriften.
Airbrushtechnik, Zeichnungen, Layouts, Fertigoriginale, Plakate, Bücher, Siebdruck.

Kirsten + Karsten Koch

Skjoldsgade 11
DK-8260 Viby J
Tel. 06-11 40 10

Retouche – Layout – Rentegning.

Carsten Madsen

Kronprinsessegade 42, st.
DK-1306 Copenhagen K
Tel. 01-13 13 11

"Carsten is a nice Aalborg-boy from March 1956. He das drawn since he was little. Now he is big and makes illustrations of almost any kind."
Carsten's mother

"Carsten er ien guer Aalbår-dræng frå mars 1956 å håer tæjnæ'lie frå haj wår bette. No æ'haj stuer, å lawwer tæjnenger å næjsten åel slaws."
Carstens muer

"Carsten er en god Aalborg-dreng fra marts 1956 og har tegnet lige fra han var lille. Nu er han stor, og laver illustrationer af næsten enhver slags."
Carstens mor

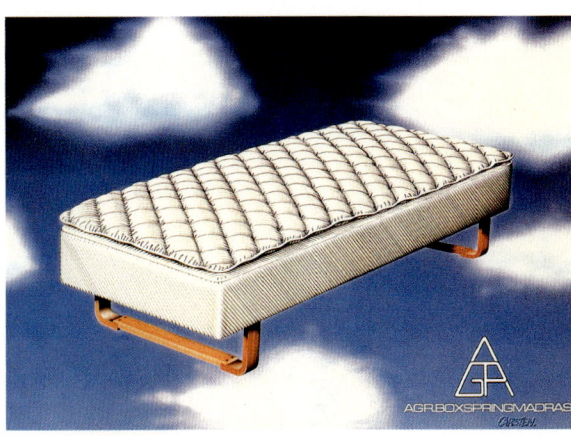

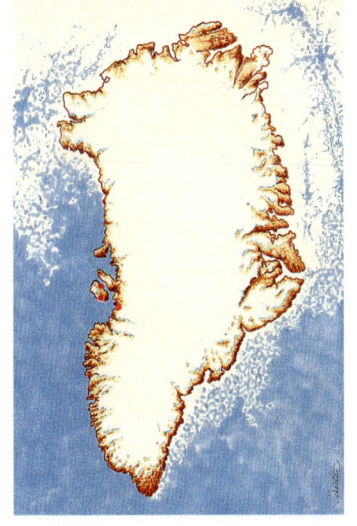

LM-ILLUSTRATION

Tuborg Havnevej 58
DK–2900 Hellerup
Tel. 451-20 11 70

Technical illustrations are our speciality!
Translates complicated technique into easily understood illustrations.
We develop, teach and work with "Computer Aided Illustration" (3-D).
Working in black and white and in colour.
Technique is fun!

Teknisk illustration er vort speciale!
Vi oversætter kompliceret teknik til letforståelige illustrationer.
Vi udvikler, underviser og arbejder med "Computer Aided Illustration" (3-D).
Arbejder i sort/hvid og farver.
Teknik er sjovt!

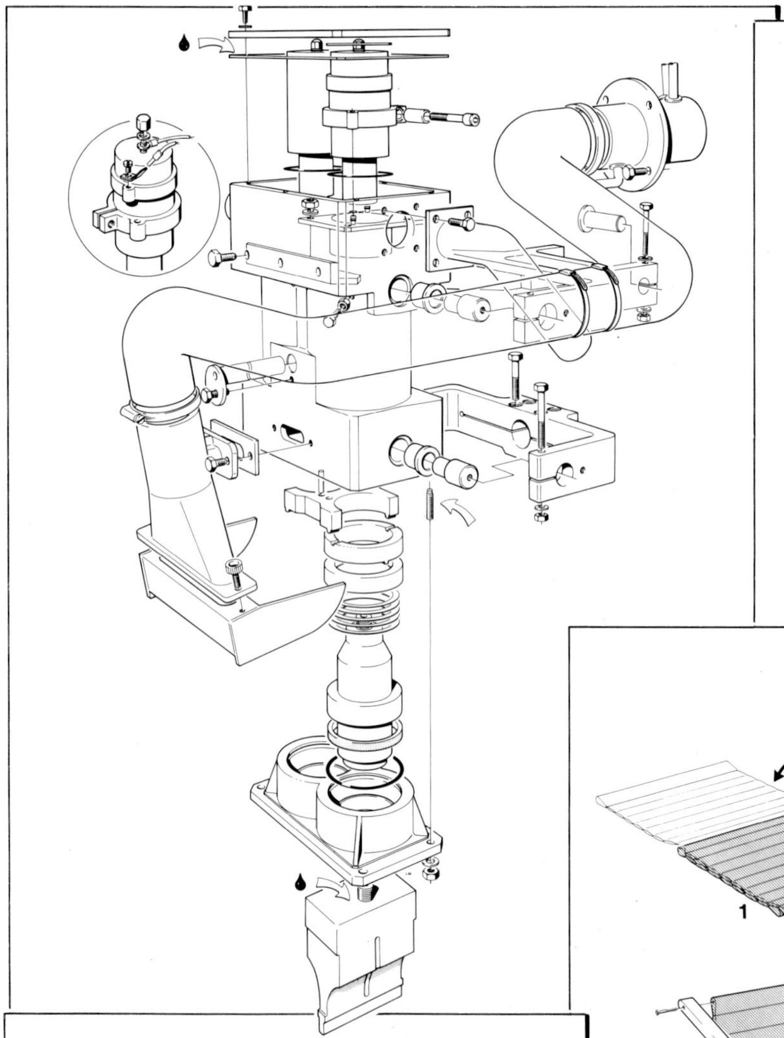

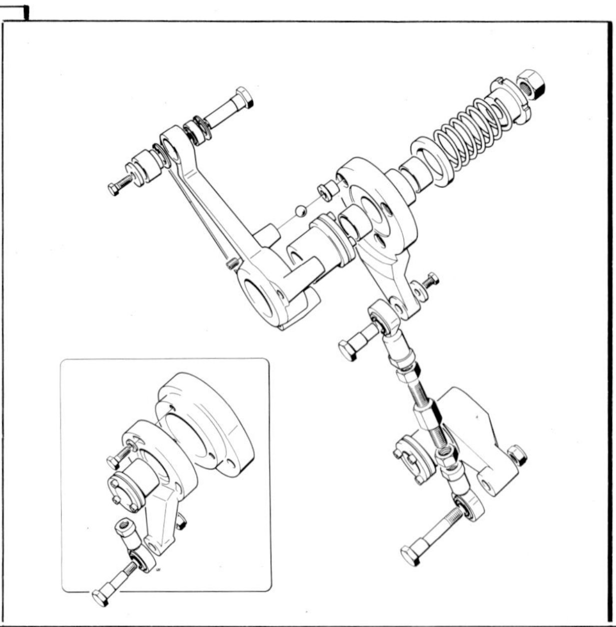

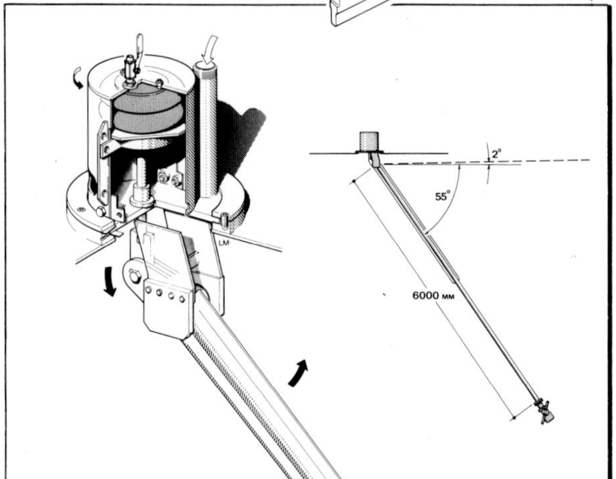

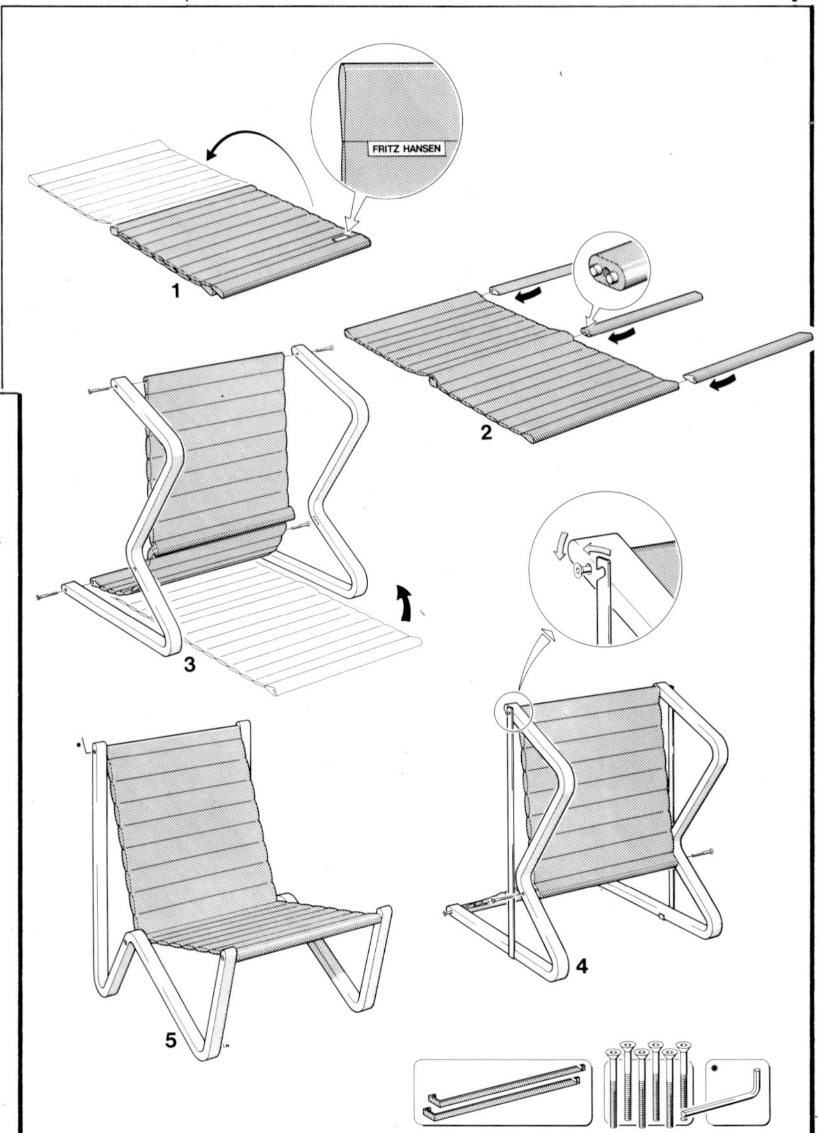

LM-ILLUSTRATION

Tuborg Havnevej 58
DK–2900 Hellerup
Tel. 451-20 11 70

Technical illustrations are our speciality!
Translates complicated technique into easily understood illustrations.
We develop, teach and work with "Computer Aided Illustration" (3-D).
Working in black and white and in colour.
Technique is fun!

Teknisk illustration er vort speciale!
Vi oversætter kompliceret teknik til letforståelige illustrationer.
Vi udvikler, underviser og arbejder med "Computer Aided Illustration" (3-D).
Arbejder i sort/hvid og farver.
Teknik er sjovt!

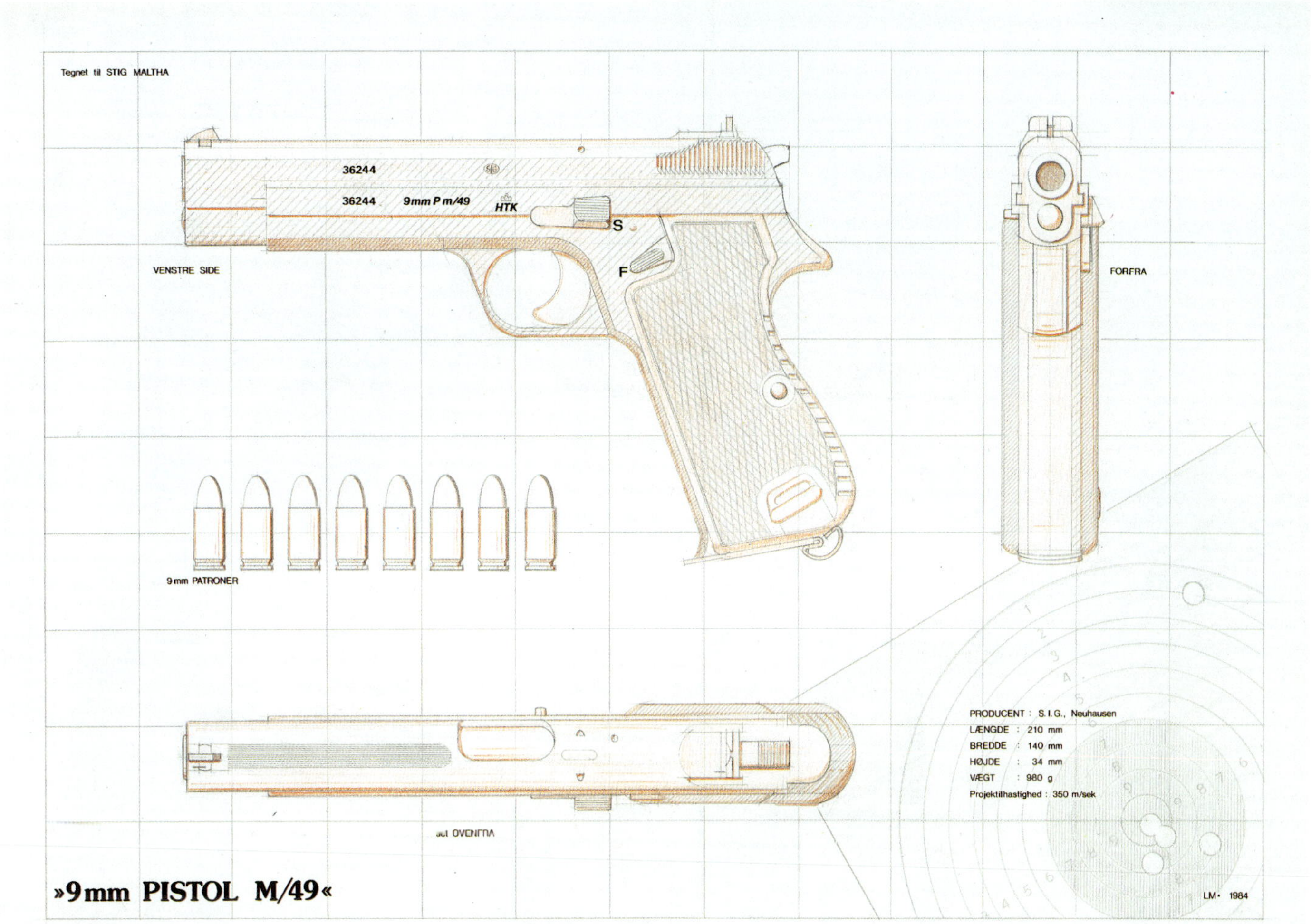

Fred Preston

Mosevej 2
DK-3450 Allerod
Tel. 02-27 18 38

London:
The Organisation
69 Caledonian Road
GB–London N1 9BT
Tel. 01-833 8268

Paris:
Vapeurs
84, boulevard Latour-Maubourg
F–75007 Paris
Tél. 45 55 53 23

Stockholm:
Kerstin Gustafsson
Kronobergsgatan 21
S–112 33 Stockholm
Tel. 08-52 06 84

ADIA 8 1987 © Fred Preston

Joe Petagno

Gl. Kongevej 87
DK-1850 Frederiksberg C
Tel. 01-21 56 05

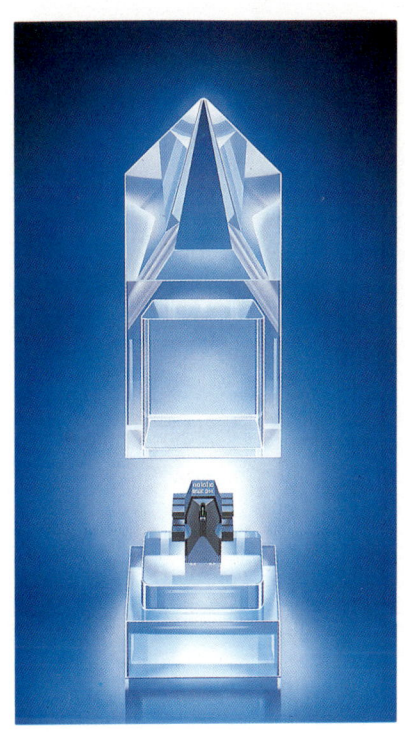

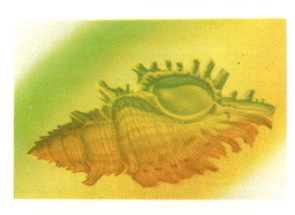

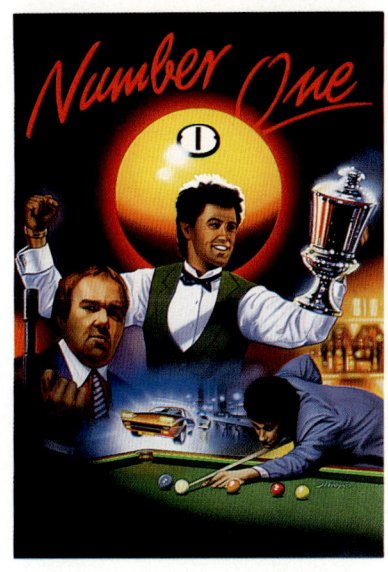

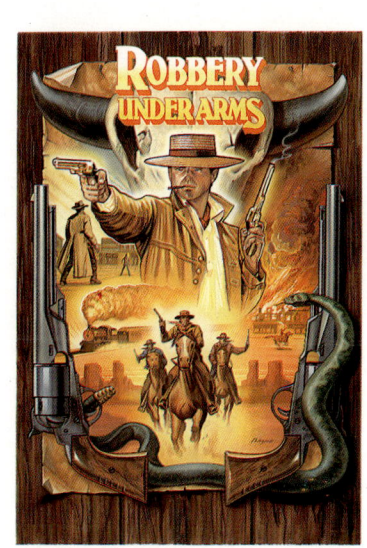

3-D Illustrations

Cut by Søren Thaae
Maglekildevej 16
DK-1853 Copenhagen
Tel. +451-31 24 42

My scissors are my pencil.

T. Oberoi

**Oberoi
Graphic Communication**

Rytterhusene 39
DK-2620 Albertslund
Tel. National 02 62 10 10
Tel. International +45 2 62 10 10

The philosophy of my work is to purify all aspects of applied art, graphic art, and the know-how of production and industrial design; and thus provide a medium for the promotion of research and creativity in the field of graphic communication.

Filosofien vedrørende mit arbejde er, at forædle alle aspekter af brugsgrafik, kunstgrafik og viden omkring produktion og industriel design – for således at tilvejebringe et middel til fremme af udvikling og kreativitet inden for området af grafisk kommunikation.

Years of international experience in effective contemporary illustrations from conception to execution. Professional photo retouching-airbrush, black & white and colour.

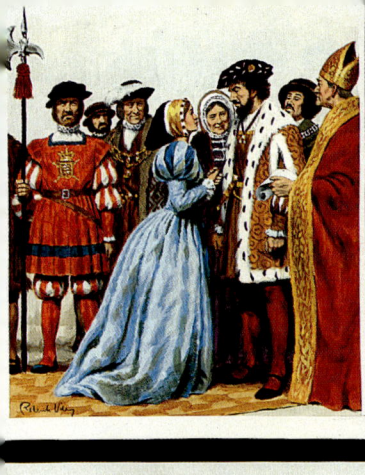

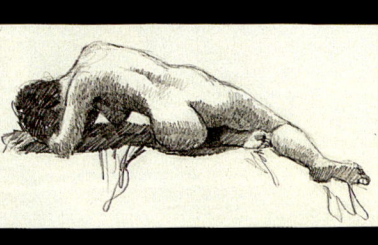

Finland
Finlande
Finnland

Gray, Stewart   270

ILLUSTRATORS

Stewart Gray

Infographics Oy
Annankatu 31-33 D. 56
SF–00100 Helsinki
Tel. 90-694 90 14

Technical and product illustration.

Illustration technique et de produits.

Technische sowie Produkt-Illustration.

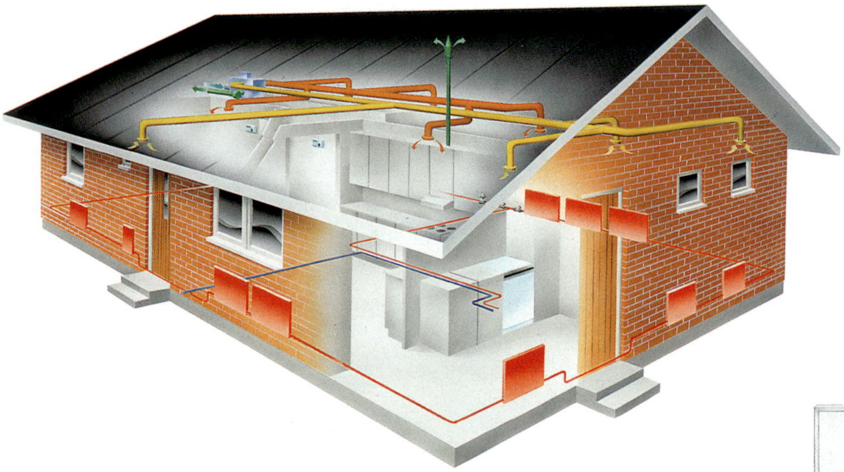

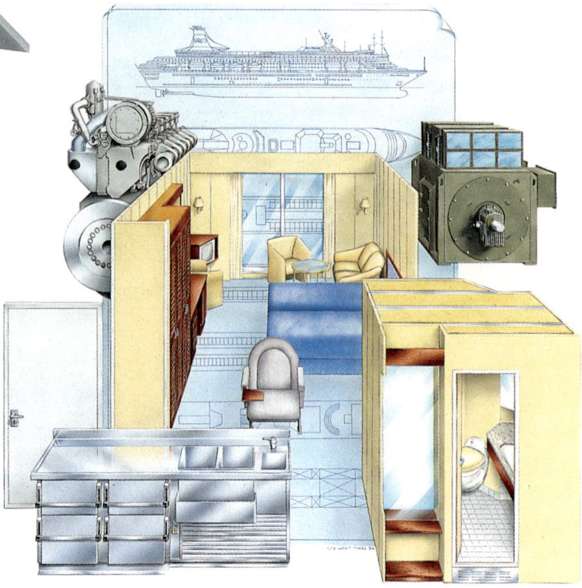

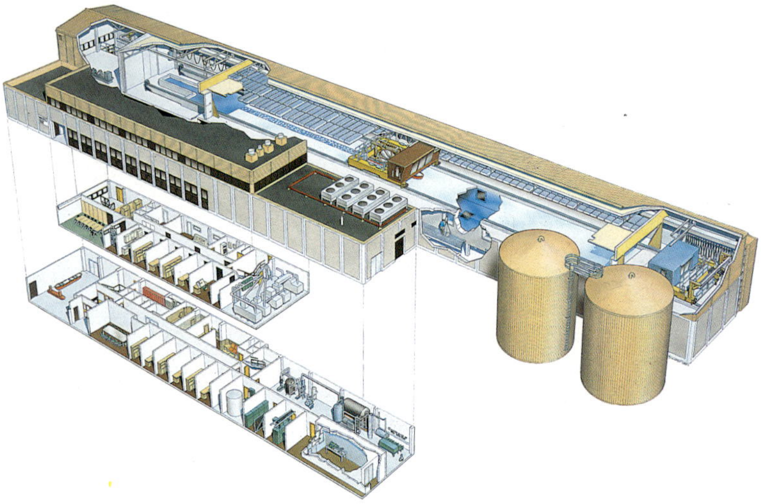

Norway
Norvège
Norwegen

Graff, Rolf 272
Malvïn, M.M. 276
Spalder, Frithjof 273
Stephansen-Smith, Kristin 274
Zibell, Volker 275

ILLUSTRATORS

Frithjof Spalder

Ymersv. 1
N-0588 Oslo 5
Tel. 22 88 61

Rolf Graff

Industrigt. 38B
N-0357 Oslo 3
Tel. 60 95 33

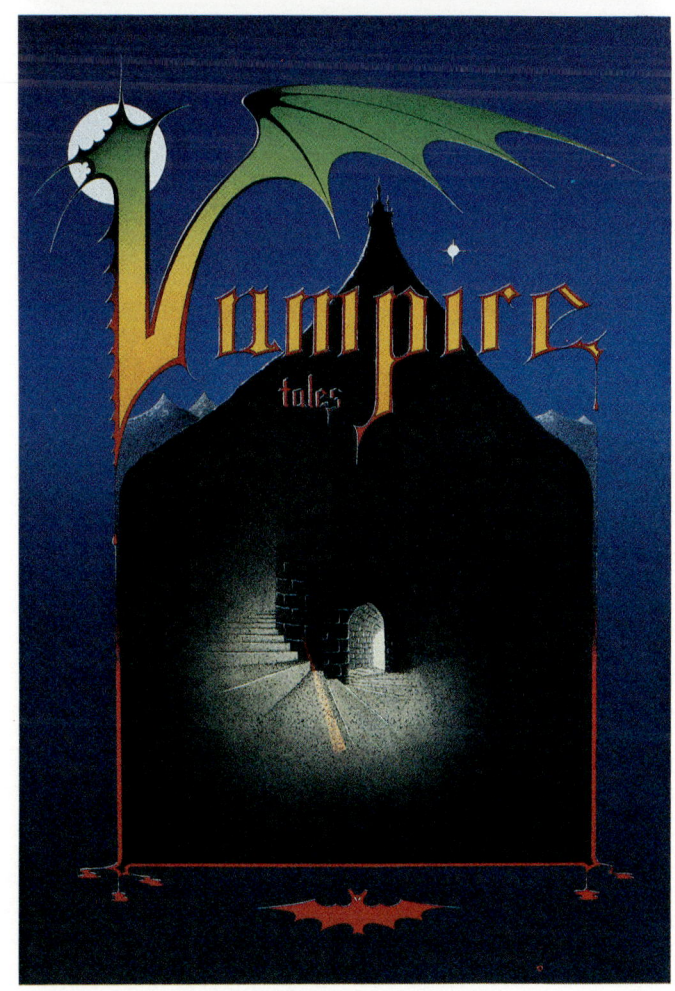

Kristin Stephansen-Smith

Box 7652 Skillebekk
N-0205 Oslo 2
Tel. 02-55 26 93
     37 47 59

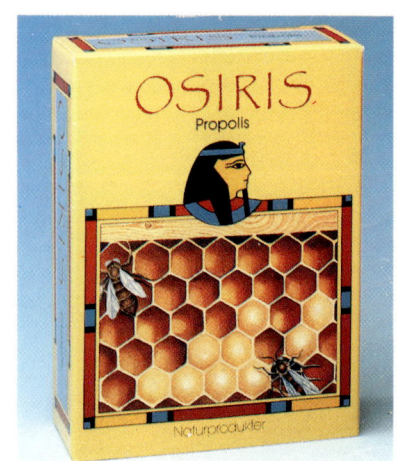
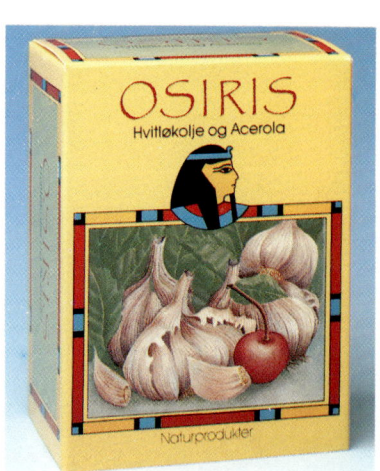

Volker Zibell

Grønnegt. 13 B
N-0350 Oslo 3
Tel. 69 89 28

Osterhausgt. 4 B
N-0183 Oslo 1
Tel. 11 18 08

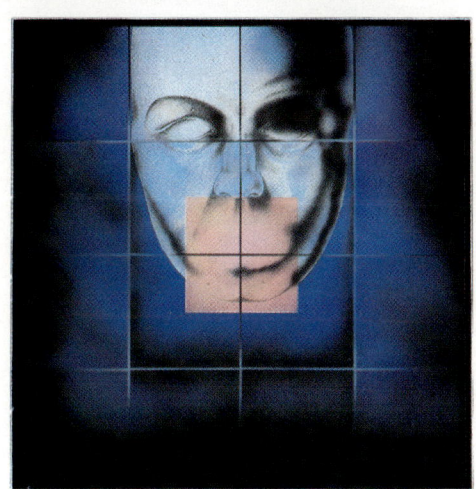

M.M. Malvin

Brochmannsgt. 3
N–0470 Oslo 4
Tel. 02-55 26 93

Sweden
Suède
Schweden

ILLUSTRATORS

Netzler, Kurt.   278-279
Trägårdh, Richard   280

Kurt Netzler

Studio 8AB
Bagartorpsringen 8
Solna – Sweden
Tel. 08-85 70 07
Fax: 08-85 13 08

Ateljen Täby:
Tel. 08-756 5100

278

Kurt Netzler

Studio 8AB
Bagartorpsringen 8
Solna – Sweden
Tel. 08-85 70 07
Fax: 08-85 13 08

Ateljen Täby:
Tel. 08-756 5100

Richard Trägårdh

Agent:
Einar Båge
Vikvägen 16
S–133 00 Saltsjöbaden
Tel. 08-717 15 24

Designer and freelance artist specialized in airbrush, oil, waterpainting. Marbel and wood imitations. All kinds of illustration and decor painting in public premises. Clients include: Swedish Space Corporation (ESRANGE), Swedish Civil Aviation Administration, Royal Academy of Natural Science, LKAB, authorities, institutions and many more.

Freischaffender Designer und Künstler, spezialisiert auf Airbrush-, Öl- und Wasserfarbenmalerei. Marmor- und Holzimitationen. Alle Arten von Illustration und Dekormalerei in öffentlichen Plätzen.

Graphiste et artiste indépendant spécialisé dans l'aérographe, l'huile, l'aquarelle. Imitations du marbre et du bois. Toutes sortes d'illustrations et décors pour lieux publics.

Spain
Espagne
Spanien

ILLUSTRATORS

Arnas, Vicente   282-283
Ballesta, Juan   286
Borja, Paul   287
Diaz Santana, Humberto   284-285
Grupo Rojo   296
Mistiano, Mauro   294

Orestis   288-289
Ramos, Eugenio   290
Riera, Joaquin   292-293
Tabernero, Manolo   291
Travieso, Miguel   295

VICENTE ARNAS

Humberto Diaz Santana
COMANDANTE ZORITA, 49 - 1º "B"
28020 MADRID • TEL. 254 50 50

JUAN BALLESTA
Puerto Rico, 11. Bajo D.
28016. Madrid
Telf. 250 77 51

Eugenio Ramos

Plaza Olavide, 5
E–28010 Madrid
Tel. 91-488 24 04

Illustrator with professional experience acquired over 28 years in such techniques as oils, acrylics, airbrush, colour pencil, pastels.

Ilustrador con experiencia profesional, adquirida durante 28 años en técnicas como óleo, acrílico, aerógrafo, lápices de color, pastel.

Clients/Clientes:
Bassat, Ogilvy & Mather, Carvis, Clarín, Contrapunto, Danis, Benton & Bowles, Delvico/Bates, Ecom, Grey, Leo Burnett, Lintas, McCann Erickson, Muga, Saatchi & Saatchi Compton, Tándem, Tapsa, Ted Bates, J.W. Thompson, Vitruvio-30, Young & Rubicam.

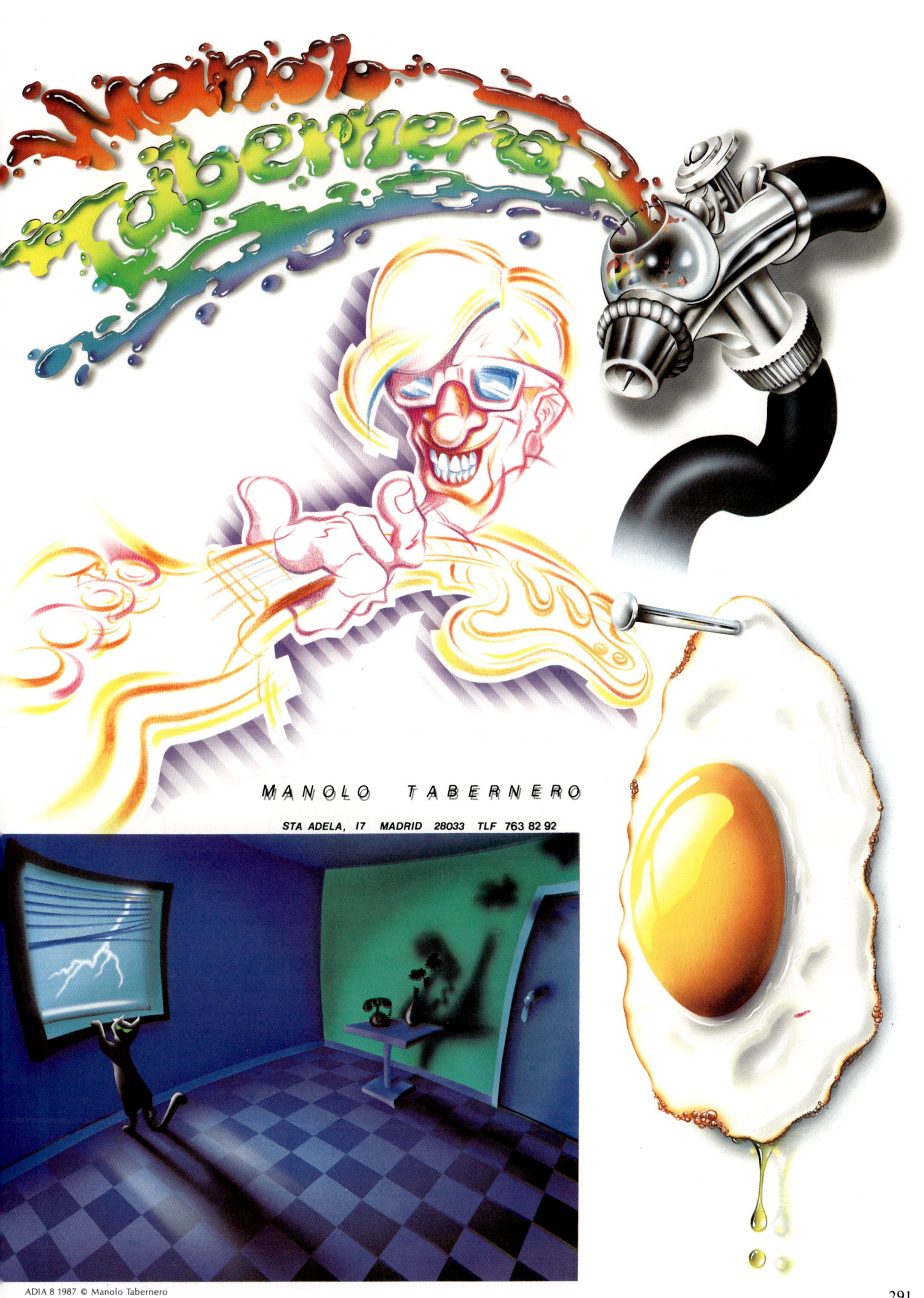

JOAQUÍN RIERA
diseño

PARA QUE TE SIENTAS LIBRE
TO MAKE YOU FEEL FREE

Boceto ilustración compresa para DAYAX
agencia de publicidad

Diseño integral de imagen de empresa
para VISUAL MARKETING

Diseño integral de imagen de empresa
para CUIN-STIL

Ilustración soporte campaña
Ventiladores KENDAL

Anuncio campaña promoción
ESTAMPACIONES SABADELL

MUY ABSORBENTE
Absorbemos cualquier tipo de trabajos con múltiples soluciones. Para que tu estés libre.

PROTEGE MAS
y mejor. Pásanos tus necesidades de diseño integral de imagen de empresa, bocetos, ilustración aerograf, arte final y olvídate.

VERY ABSORBENT
We absorb any type of jobs with a multiplicity of solutions. So you will be free.

IT PROTECTS MORE
and better. Pass onto us your needs in total company image design, sketches, aerographic illustrations, final artwork, and forget about it.

Joaquin Riera

Rosellón, 231 Pral. 2ª
08008 Barcelona
Tel.: 217 14 24

ADIA 8 1987 © Joaquin Riera

293

DIBUJANTE · ILUSTRADOR

Gral. Alvarez de Castro, 43 - Bajo Dcha.
Telf. 445 07 77 - 28010 MADRID

miguel travieso · Pza. de la Cruz 3 , 47162 - Aldeamayor de S. Martín (Valladolid) ; Tlf. (983) 55 69 51

Diseño · Ilustración GRUPO ROJO

calle Gramíneas, 3, urbanización La Grajilla · San Sebastian de los Reyes
28609 · Madrid, Teléfono, (91) 654 46 49

1.987 video producciones VALFER

1.987 VIDEO SERVICE, s.a.

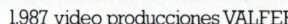

1.987 video producciones VALFER

ILLUSTRATORS

United Kingdom
Grande-Bretagne
Grossbritannien

Artists Inc. Ltd   298
Beard, Terry   299
Chamberlain, John   301
Harfield, Mark   300
Industrial Art Studio   302
Pinkbarge   306-307

Tiner, Ron   303
Towns Artworks, Lynn   304-305
Vaughan, Mike   308-309
VENUS Family, The   310
Winn, Chris   311
Young Artists   312

Artists Inc. Ltd

15 Stukeley Street
Covent Garden
London WC2B 5LT
Tel. 01-405 0355

Contact:
Paul Reeves

Artists featured, left to right:
Heather James; Mark Rowney;
Jonathan Minshull; John Spires;
Andrew Sutcliffe; Peter Harris;
Martin White; Ian Bott;
Marc Woodhouse.

Also representing:
Peter Beavis; Jean Foster;
James Griffiths; Barry Jones;
Elizabeth Kerr; Tracey Kleinman;
Phil Littler; Joanna Venus.

Terry Beard

The Old Police House
Devizes Road
Upavon
Pewsey
Wilts SN9 6ED
Tel. 0980-630177

Agent:
Maggie Mundy
216 King Street
London W6 0RA
Tel. 01-741 5862

General illustration.
Past clients include:
BBC Books, Usborne Publishing, Athena International, British Home Stores, IPC Magazines, Second Nature, Cambridge University Press.

Mark Harfield

176 Haverstock Hill
London NW3 2AL
Tel. 01-480 5168
     794 4089

New York
Tel. 718-388 9055

For a 'bunch of information', see "Creative Review", March 1987 issue. Inside is a three page profile on the work of Mark Harfield and his company 'Bunch of Artists'.

Pour de plus amples informations, veuillez consulter le numéro de «Creative Review» de mars 1987. Trois pages sont consacrées aux travaux de Mark Harfield et de son agence 'Bunch of Artists'.

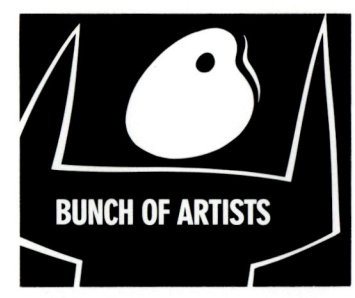

BUNCH OF ARTISTS

John Chamberlain

14 Telston Close
Bourne End
Bucks SL8 5TY
Tel. 06285-21941

Industrial Art Studio

Roger Full / Industrial Art Studio
Consols
St. Ives
Cornwall TR26 2HW
Tel. 0736-797651
Fax: 0736-794291

Agent for Sweden:
Roberts Long & Co. AB
Nya Torg 11
S–243 00 Höör
Tel. 010-46-413-24008

Technical line and airbrush illustrations.
Artwork for consumer goods advertising and packaging.

Illustrations techniques au trait et à l'aérographe.
Réalisations publicitaires et créations d'emballages pour des produits de consommation courante.

Technische Illustrationen mit Federstrich und Aerograf.
Realisierung von Reklamen, sowie Entwürfe von Verpackungen für geläufige Verbrauchsprodukte.

Ron Tiner

1 Gordon Road
Exeter
Devon EX1 2DH
Tel. 0392-213066

General fiction, fantasy, historical, editorial, advertising and industrial illustration.
Comic strips.

Illustration de fiction générale, fantastique, historique, éditoriale, publicitaire et industrielle.
Bandes dessinées.

Illustration für Romane, Märchen, Geschichtliches, Verlagsprodukte, Werbung und Industrie.
Comic strips.

Lynn Towns Artworks

92 Kimberley Road
Penylan
Cardiff CF2 5DN
Tel. 0222-498605

Artists featured, left to right:
Jerry Hoare
Sarah Hopkins
Sal Garfi (centre)
Clare Stroud
Debi Gliori
Jenny Fagence

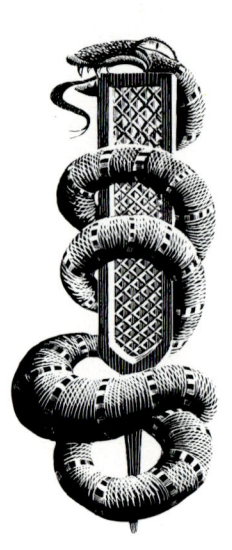

Lynn Towns Artworks

92 Kimberley Road
Penylan
Cardiff CF2 5DN
Tel. 0222-49 86 05

Artists featured, left to right:
Paul Simpkins
Mark Burton – Trust House Forte
Siân Davies
Debi Gliori
Ieuan Rees – lettering and calligraphy
Ieuan Rees
Mark James – Grant and Partners
Jenny Beck

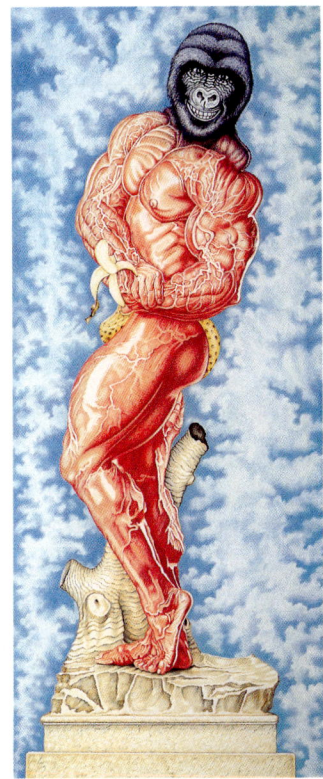

pinkbarge

17 DE WALDEN STREET, LONDON W1M 7PJ
TEL: 01 486 1053 · 01 935 1906 · 01 935 2417

Neil McDonald

Jan Hill

Alec Hitchins

John Beswick

Mike Vaughan

Roy Taylor

Bob Heindel

pinkbarge
17 DE WALDEN STREET, LONDON W1M 7PJ
TEL: 01 486 1053 · 01 935 1906 · 01 935 2417

Kate Osborne

Andrew Bale

Milanda Lopez

Jack McCarthy

Jon Blake

Jane Thomson

Lynne Dennis

Mike Vaughan

216 Sheen Lane
East Sheen
London SW14 8LB
Tel. 01-876 9260

Agents:
Pinkbarge
17 De Walden Street
London W1M 7PJ
Tel. 01-486 1053

The Art Box
Weesperzijde 85
NL–1091 EJ Amsterdam
Tel. 020-68 15 51

Roberts Long & Co. AB
Nya Torg 11
S–243 00 Höör – Sweden
Tel. +46-413-2 40 08

Mike Vaughan

216 Sheen Lane
East Sheen
London SW14 8LB
Tel. 01-876 9260

Agents:
Pinkbarge
17 De Walden Street
London W1M 7PJ
Tel. 01-486 1053

The Art Box
Weesperzijde 85
NL–1091 EJ Amsterdam
Tel. 020-68 15 51

Roberts Long & Co. AB
Nya Torg 11
S–243 00 Höör – Sweden
Tel. +46-413-2 40 08

The VENUS Family

Contact at either:
63 Wimbourne House
Dorset Road
London SW8 1AJ
Tel. 01-582 2633

or:
Whin Brow Cottage
Hood Lane
Cloughton
Nr. Scarborough
N. Yorkshire YO13 0AT
Tel. 0723-87 08 73

Top images: Pamela Venus

Middle images: Sarah Venus

Bottom images: Joanna Venus

Chris Winn FCSD

40 Taverham Road
Drayton
Norwich
Norfolk NR8 6RY
Tel. 0603-860532
Fax: 0603-860532

Cover illustration for Bristol & West Building Society "Savers Guide".

Young Artists

2 Greenland Place
London NW1 0AP
Tel. 01-267 9661
Fax: 01-267 9663

Representing 40 illustrators.
Catalogue available.

ANDREA NORTON

NATALIE CROUCH

ANDRE YANIW

LYNNE ROBINSON

JOHN CLEMENTSON

JENNY TYLDEN WRIGHT

JANET WOOLLEY

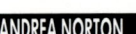
JANE HUMAN

NIGEL CHAMBERLAIN

LES EDWARDS

YOUR ELECTRONIC NOTEBOOK

PHILIPS POCKET MEMO

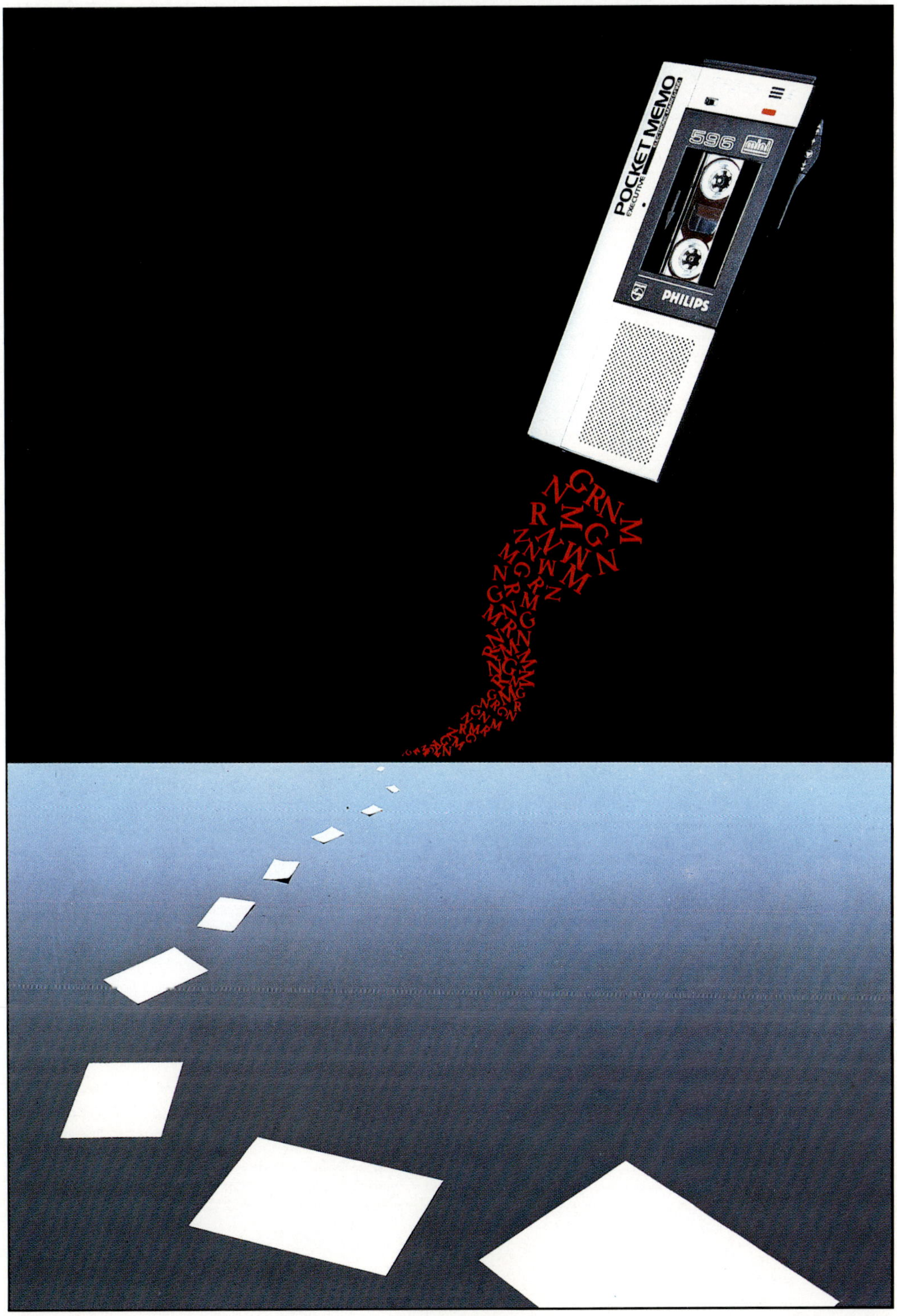

Philips Pocket Memo is sold throughout the USA under the NORELCO brand name

You've chosen a fast moving business where everything happens at once. With no time to write, no time to get your ideas, notes and reminders onto paper, there's so much that can go wrong. That's why you need the speed and convenience of a Philips Pocket Memo – your electronic notebook. You can take it everywhere. It's instant, compact and always ready for use. Try one out for yourself. You'll soon wonder how you ever managed to get through the day without it.

THE WORLD'S NO. 1 IN DICTATION

For more information write to: Philips Desk Equipment, Triester Strasse 64, A-1101, Vienna, Austria.

PHILIPS

HEAR THE DIFFERENCE Just as your ears can instantly pick up a bum note, they can
by science or flashing lights – all you have to do is listen. Our dealers will be pleased to
Your ears will hear music like they've never heard before. For further information contact

MOST HI-FI SYSTEMS

tell when one hi-fi system sounds better than another. So don't be blinded
let you hear Linn equipment and compare the sound with other systems.
Linn Products, Floors Rd., Eaglesham, Glasgow G76 0PX, Tel: (041) 644 5111.

LINN
HIGH FIDELITY
YOU'VE NEVER HEARD IT
SO GOOD.

LINN HI-FI SYSTEM

THE MORE THE BETTER.

Tipp-Ex fluid Super Set.

DESIGNER CAMERA.

Take it in style.

Whatever's in fashion catch it with the new Image System camera from Polaroid. You can take just one picture at a time and check your reference right on the spot. No other camera can do this.

With fully automatic functions, a revolutionary lens, bright new colours and a built-in flash, it's been designed to make instant visual notes.

The Image camera is part of a system which includes optional accessories such as tripod, camera bag, album and filter kit.

You can take the compact Image System anywhere and it's faster than a Filofax.

Add it to your collection now.

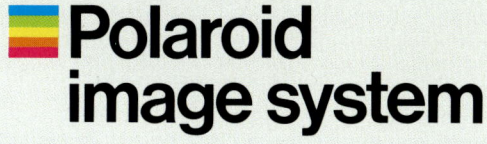

'Polaroid' is a regd. trademark of the Polaroid Corporation, Mass., USA.

AGFA FILMS. PREFERRED BY THOSE WHO KNOW.

GERHARD VORMWALD

photographed Francis Giacobetti on Agfachrome 100 RS Professional roll film using a Rolleiflex 6006.

This is what Gerhard Vormwald said about his portrait: Francis creates pictures of women with a geometric quality. I wanted to carry this idea of geometry into my photograph. I decided to show a girl's body in relation to Francis. She is floating weightlessly over Francis, who is picturing her in his mind.
I chose the fine-grained Agfachrome 100 RS for this shot. The film sensitively separates the monochrome areas, and renders even minute detail razor-sharp. These are the characteristics that enabled me to bring off this daring composition.

<u>Agfa Professional: 35 mm and roll films for slides (ISO 50–1000) and colour negatives (ISO 100–1000).</u>

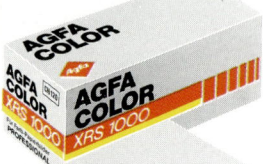

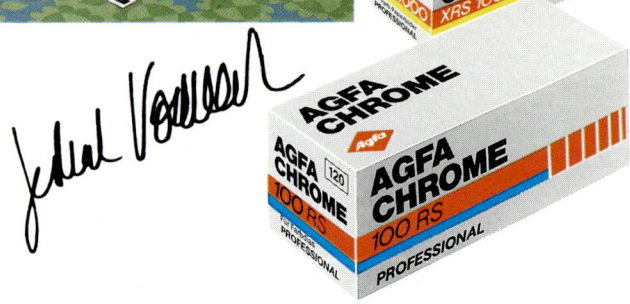

BASF Professional
Audio · Video

For further information contact:

BASF United Kingdom Limited
BASF House
151 Wembley Park Drive
GB-Wembley
Middlesex
HA9 8JG
Tel (1) 9 08 31 88
Telefax (1) 9 08 58 66
Telex 269 451 basf lo g

BASF Aktiengesellschaft
Unternehmensbereich
Informationssysteme
Gottlieb-Daimler-Straße 10
Postfach 51 46
D-6800 Mannheim 1
Tel (06 21) 60-0
Telefax (06 21) 60-4 43 95
Telex 46 499-0 bas d

A full range of products available for all applications.

Tapes for Radio, Television, Duplicators, Sound and Film Recording.